Just Barbara

Just Barbara

An autobiography by
BARBARA WOODHOUSE

Published by Michael Joseph and Rainbird

First published in Great Britain in 1981 by
Michael Joseph Ltd
44 Bedford Square
London WC1
and
George Rainbird Ltd
36 Park Street
London W1
who designed and produced the book

© Barbara Woodhouse 1981

ISBN 0 7181 2012 4

Printed and bound by
W. S. Cowell Ltd, Ipswich, Suffolk

Contents

Early days

The first thing I remember clearly at the age of eighteen months is the birth of my baby sister, Hazel. A maternity nurse of ample proportions took over our nursery. She wore a navy blue dress and a long starched apron which, owing to its prickly stiffness, would have effectively kept one from hugging her, even if one had wanted to. What fascinated me most about her were her rosy cheeks surmounted by a frilly white bonnet cap tied under her chin. I clearly remember her bringing 'your new baby sister' down the stairs leading to our nursery and sitting before the roaring log fire with a bundle so wrapped in starched white garments and a huge woollen shawl that, at first, I saw no sister at all. On peeping closer I saw a mass of black straight hair surrounding a tiny little face; she was fast asleep. I tried to touch her but was gently pushed back by Nurse Kite and told 'just to look' which seemed to me to be an awfully dull thing to do with a new sister, so I went off to play with Nanny and my other sister, Nadine (Dene for short), who was eighteen months older than me. We both had dolls and lots of toy animals. Dene had a lovely doll with big eyes, real hair and lots of clothes all of which could be

OPPOSITE *At two years old I was bored with the photographer!*

7

taken off, washed and put back. I had a rather inferior doll which I called Vera after my aunt, but my favourite toy was Beeky Bar, a duck made of lots of coloured pieces of felt with boot buttons as eyes. Even at this early age I preferred animals, and it was lucky for us, especially for me, that Nanny was also an animal lover, for our nursery always housed some sick animal, a bird with a broken wing or a rabbit with a chill.

I soon lost interest in my new sister as she did not want to play and she made horrible screaming noises. I do not know why but it remains very clearly in my mind that at that particular time I was in the way, everyone seemed busy fussing over the new sister. My mother lay in bed with her golden hair spread all over the pillow, and she did not get up for our playtime, which was normally at five o'clock, after tea, when we were dressed in our very best party clothes and taken down to the drawing-room for an hour. Now we did not do this; we stayed upstairs in the nursery or went and sat on Mummy's bed while she read to us, but I could not sit still for long and went back to Nanny in the nursery who was always willing to play and did not seem to pay much attention to the new baby sister. I am sure that it was this memory of a new baby being a hindrance to my normal existence which made me 'hate babies' in my early days.

The nursery wing at St Columba's College, Rathfarnham, Co. Dublin, the boys' public school where my father was headmaster, was at the top of the very large headmaster's house. An enormously wide flight of stone steps led to it. Half-way up was a large window looking out onto the beautiful flower border and lawns of which my mother was so fond. A large breeding cage for Nanny's canaries and a smaller cage for my sister's budgerigars hung from this window. Dene had taught her two budgerigars innumerable tricks, as well as talking, such as picking a card from a pack of fortune-telling cards.

OPPOSITE ABOVE *Dene, myself and Hazel with
'Mrs Wyandotte' at St Columba's*
BELOW *Sitting on the steps of St Columba's with Hazel*

The birds were tame and used to fly about in our nursery but although very lovable, I was far more interested in animals.

The first nine years of my life were spent at St Columba's with my two sisters and brother. We were brought up in this glorious place with one hundred and fifty acres of woods and moorland behind us and a long-distance view of the sea. We had two dogs, a large rough Collie called Sandy and a little black Pomeranian called Jim, both of whom lived in the nursery. Jim followed us everywhere but Sandy was too big to come with us on the daily afternoon pony trap outings Mother considered essential for our health. It did not matter what the weather was like we still had to go out. In freezing weather, Jim would lie on the floor under the large waterproof rug lined with navy blue wool which covered us all up and he would keep our feet warm. Nanny always drove the pony although after my fourth birthday she would let me take the reins. I loved the pony and, much to the displeasure of the groom, was forever feeding it sugar, even when it was waiting at the front door to take us all on our drive. In those days the bits were made of steel and took a lot of burnishing which was made harder by the sugary mess left on the bit! Our ponies were always being changed. They came from the local horse-dealer on a week's trial. This Irish dealer knew which side his bread was buttered on and, if we did not like the pony or it had some vice like shying, he would bring another always just that much more expensive until, in the end, my father was paying an exorbitant price to get the right pony. However, we finally did get a lovely little bay pony and, when I was five, I drove it myself each day to Dundrum to fetch our governess. Once we met an enormous steamroller re-surfacing the road and the pony would not go past this monster. One of the road-workers had to lead the pony along the road but once past, it went like the wind. The pony and I had a great rapport and the faster it went, the happier I was. My governess was not so sure she liked this and was always asking me to slow down but I paid no attention.

This pony was only for the trap. The whole family was taught to ride at a very early age on 'Pamela', Mother's black

Riding Pamela, Mother's black donkey

donkey which she had had as a girl and which was very old. When I was two, I was put on it in a sort of saddle basket to which I was strapped and led about. It was not long before I was telling Nanny to let go, I wanted to ride alone. Pamela seemed to sense my happiness for she was quite willing to go where I wanted which was up and down the drive leading to our house. Later on, I had a grey donkey of my own who had a baby donkey. We called them Bluebell and Violet and when I was about six, I 'broke in' Violet who was then about eighteen months old. I got on her first by climbing on a box at the side whilst Hazel held her on a head collar. We had no saddle to fit such a tiny donkey. Then it was Hazel's turn to climb up and I ran up and down with her. Hazel was three years old then. She and I were the only members of the family to really enjoy riding. Charlie, my eldest brother, loathed it but in those days in Ireland, everyone rode as a matter of course, and he had to learn like the rest of us. He was terrified of cantering and fell off several times despite the fact that we had a lovely quiet bay pony. I think the pony probably sensed his nerves.

During the Irish rebellion of 1916, we were out one afternoon in the pony trap when the groom came rushing up on one of the work horses and told Nanny to drive back to the college as quickly as she could. He had heard that we were on the list of those to be murdered by the Sinn Feiners because we were English. On our return to the college, we learned that there had been a raid on the armoury where the guns the boys used in the army training school corps were stored and all of them had been stolen. That evening we watched the main post office in Dublin burn down through my father's telescope on the roof of the college. We thought it very exciting!

Every morning, we had lessons in a big study where the walls were covered with ancient tapestries of great value and there was an old piano in one corner. Our lessons were run on PNEU (Parents National Education Union) lines and I remember how bored I was having painstakingly to write 'beautiful' script. I am sure this is why my writing is so bad today. When we had to go to another school I had to learn to write all over again, this time joining up the letters! Our governesses came and left with such regularity that it was difficult to keep up with them. We were five high spirited children and always got up to tricks. I say five because Charlie, my elder brother, was rather shy and Mother and Father thought he should have a companion of his own age to bring him out so Willie Telford, a relative of the famous organ makers, was brought into our family circle. He was an outgoing boy, red-headed and freckled, full of fun and quite lovely to live with. Charlie and he became great friends. One day, I remember Charlie and Willie climbing onto the roof of the 'boot shed' where the school 'boot boy' cleaned all the boys' boots. The governess, who was then a Miss Pattison, had to pass by this shed on leaving the pony trap to get to our schoolroom; she was a prim lady in whose eyes we could do nothing right so we were always up to pranks. This time she got more

*Willie Telford
and Dene*

Charlie on his sledge

than she expected as Charlie and Willie had hauled the garden hose up onto the roof, pretending to wash it down, and completely soaked her when she passed underneath. Despite their abject apologies, Miss Pattison left on the spot!

The next governess was a gentle Miss Wand, whom we all liked and, at last, our education progressed. In fact she was the one who suggested the boys build a hut in the park adjoining the college so that, in hot weather, we could have our lessons

Dene, Hazel and myself by the school hut

there. This really endeared her to us all and, when the hut was finished and the crevices filled with moss, we used to go there for our lessons, right up to the end of September, if the weather was fine.

One of the things that fascinated me about Miss Wand was the succulent way she had of eating her elevenses which was brought to her on a dainty tray by one of the school maids. This always consisted of two thin heavily buttered slices of white bread, a tiny china pot of tea, milk and sugar. When she ate the bread, her lips became moist which made the thin slices of bread and butter seem all the more tasty. I always felt hungry just watching her and wondered why we never got elevenses. I, for one however, did not need them for I loved my food and would have got far too fat, not that the college food was appetising, just filling. The school food sent up from the kitchen to the nursery in a lift was typical of boys' meals in those days: spotted dog, figs, bread and butter pudding . . . Nanny was very strict with us, never allowing us to get down from table until we had left a clean plate. I have sat from lunch until tea time in front of a plate of baked custard and figs or prunes knowing that I would be sick if I ate either one of them. I tried hiding the figs under the handles of my spoon and fork but Nanny always found me out. If I remember rightly I was eventually allowed to leave the uneatable offering by tea time.

I was Nanny's favourite in spite of the fact that I was the naughtiest of the family. One day, as a punishment for some naughtiness, she put me in the corner by a large curtain which hung from the window. Her knitting bag was dangling on a hook behind the curtain and by the time I was allowed out of the corner, I had unravelled a large piece of knitting. I got a smacking for this but we were rarely punished in this way as Nanny loved us dearly. She must have worked like a slave to have looked after the five of us as well as making all our clothes. She only had one day off a month and was paid forty pounds a year. In those days babies were fed twice in the night, how she managed, I don't know. Her first position had been with Sir Henry Wood looking after his children. When they no longer needed a nanny she came to us where she stayed until we were grown up.

We really loved Nanny more than our mother or father at that time because our parents were distant, slightly terrifying people whom we only saw after tea for an hour when we went down to the drawing-room. There my mother played endless games like ludo and halma with us; or read books to us. Everything was for our enjoyment, yet somehow with me it failed. I remember the card games when, at an early age, I realized that if I cheated, my mother would get extremely angry and send me out of the drawing-room back upstairs to Nanny. This was exactly what I wanted. The lectures on how I should end up in hell-fire if I cheated had little effect, although every Sunday after tea the Bible was read to us by my father who was a clergyman as well as headmaster. He always chose rather lurid passages from the Bible which should have put the fear of cheating or any other sin firmly into our minds, but as the Bible also says our sins would be forgiven, I could not see why we were supposed to be so frightened of burning in Hell. Even today, I fail utterly to understand religion. I cannot see how God can possibly sort us out when we get to the gates of Heaven or Hell. Surely the sins we commit everyday of our lives, like saying unkind things, or envying those with more possessions than we have, cannot be easily judged against those of say, child murderers? Now I prefer not to think about it. I have a code which I have set myself of trying to say sorry every night before the sun goes down to those I have hurt. I try to help those who need my help, but beyond that, I claim nothing. I do not go to church because I can pray better in the fields. I wrote a hymn called 'By Your Side' which has been published and just about sums up my views on religion: which is however much life hurts you, God is there to help you if you need Him. I do not believe prayers always get answered, I shall never comprehend why God allows such terrible things to happen to one in this life if He is all loving, yet perhaps it is for His profit and loss account and I trust and believe in Him. Three times in my life I have nearly died, and each time I felt at complete peace with no fear at all. This must be of comfort to anyone fearing death.

Early childhood memories were always those of getting on the right side of people. I was a very happy child, and I loved all people, no one was my enemy. This faith in people led me into all sorts of queer situations; there was the old thief of a butler in our household who stole biscuits and whisky, and when I was about eight, he invited me into his pantry to taste a nip of the 'strong stuff'. It nearly choked me and from that day I have never liked drink. In fact even one glass of champagne goes straight to my head and makes me giddy, so if I am at a wedding, I seldom take more than a tiny sip and then palm it off onto my husband.

After my father died, and I was only nine at the time, I always acted as intermediary between my mother and irritable tradespeople. Mother came from a long line of ancestors

*My father,
the Rev. William
Blackburn*

My mother

who in the old days would have been called 'the ruling classes'. Her crest was an arm and a hand holding a whip, and her maiden name was Masterman. I often wonder whether the family had originally been horse-trainers or dog-trainers – or were we slave traders? Mother never seemed to think that regulations were made for her and her terrific charm usually surmounted all obstacles, but occasionally a little inside help smoothed her path. I think she never accepted the word 'can't' and I have inherited this, defeat is something I have never learned to accept. Unfortunately one cannot always win, and most of my sleepless nights, of which I have many, are spent trying to solve the insoluble.

I do not seem to need much sleep at night now and therefore was not unduly annoyed when at 1.30 a.m. a lady from Bournemouth rang to learn how to house-train her dog. When I pointed out that it was the middle of the night and I had been asleep for three hours she remarked, 'Oh I do not go to bed very early!' I felt a little irritated at that remark.

Bed to me has always seemed purgatory because at the age of sixteen I seriously injured my back playing hockey and slipped a disc. That is why, for the whole of my life, except to have children, I have never spent one single day in bed through illness. If I am ill, which has only happened twice in forty years, being a speed reader, I can read as many as three books a day sitting by the fire. I have the odd feeling that if I have flu the best thing to do is to wrap up, get out into the cold and not give the germs the comfort of hot drinks, hot-water bottles and warmth. They soon find a more comfortable body to invade! Because all my life I have had animals that do not understand that 'walkies' in the woods with a high temperature is not perhaps what the doctor ordered, and because cows cannot remain unmilked, I have built up this 'mind over matter' resistance to illness.

I found being capable of speed reading of enormous use to me in my life as I have had books sent to me for review at 9 a.m. in the morning and they have gone back with a report at 11 a.m. Now I seldom read a book as I am always too exhausted. If I happen to sit down, I fall asleep especially if the television is on. I rarely ever watch a complete programme.

To go back to my early life I often wonder how much is mapped out years and years ahead, and think of the funny coincidences that happen. I well remember our early days at the Irish school where the first years of our lives were spent, the happy carefree years in an atmosphere of rigid discipline, lots of joyful entertainment and education in its widest sense. We were taught to dance, to play the piano, to act, to speak correctly . . . We had painting lessons every Wednesday with Miss Yeats, W. B. Yeats' sister. We would spend two hours painting, mostly flowers in pots, or hawthorn on brown paper which looked very nice if you had an aptitude for this sort of painting. Hazel and Dene did, and eventually, Hazel became a very good artist, Dene preferring watercolour sketches. I did not shine at all and was considered quite unteachable. I was not even corrected for my appalling paintings, and it was a complete waste of Miss Yeats' time. Charlie did not want to paint in watercolours in spite of the fact that he showed great artistic promise and, as he wished to draw in pastels or crayons, William Orpen, later Sir William Orpen, came to the college once a week to give him lessons. At one time we had innumerable sketches by this famous artist lying about. He once brought Augustus John up to the college for the day and he did a beautiful sketch of Charlie which for years lay in the loft of our house at Oxford. What it would be worth today I do not know but I think it got thrown away when the loft was cleared.

Ballet was also part of my sisters' and my education. Every Saturday we were taken to a dancing school in Dublin and fitted out with ballet shoes. We were expected to be graceful on the tips of our toes and to move our legs in a way I am sure nature never intended me to move mine. My toes just bent backwards and nearly touched my heels every time I stood on

OVERLEAF *Being a large family helped when it came to playing cricket*

my points. The mistress gave me up after about six lessons and told Mother she was wasting her money. Dene and Hazel carried on and Hazel eventually became a lovely ballet dancer on the stage.

Etiquette and behaviour at home and in public formed a big part of our education. Every Sunday, Mother and Father would invite about twelve boys to tea in the drawing-room. There would be four boys to each small table and Dene, Hazel and I would act as hostesses. We were taught to keep the 'ball rolling', never to allow the conversation to lapse into awkward, lengthy pauses and Mother would come round to each table to see how we were getting on. She had been brought up in St Petersburg where my grandfather had been an English banker and, in those days, an understanding of protocol and good behaviour was a requisite in high society. Mother taught us to encourage the boys to talk about themselves, about their interests and not to monopolise the conversation ourselves. Above all, we were taught to see that no one however drab, was left out of the party, so that they didn't enjoy themselves. This early training has left me with a basic security in public that has served me well. It made sure that we never thought of our own feelings in public and forgot our own shortcomings when talking to people, as it was the other person who mattered. It gave us a friendly outlook because we had been told that, however forbidding the exterior, there is always something worth finding in everyone.

Once a week, we were taught ballroom dancing. We learned the polka, the waltz, the hornpipe and the schottische. Again, the younger members of the school partnered us, arriving in their best suits, their hair smarmed down with dreadful hair oil. It was my misfortune one afternoon to partner one young boy who had come dressed in a brown velvet suit which had the horrible smell that corduroy used to carry, and his hair was covered in coconut oil. However, in spite of these small irritations, we certainly learned to dance and, in later years, Hazel and I taught ballroom dancing ourselves. Michael Foot and his brother, Dingle, were two of our pupils.

Some years later, when we moved to Oxford and the Christmas parties became numerous, these dancing lessons were a great help. In those days, at parties, one had little programme cards with a tiny pencil attached by a coloured cord with a fluffy piece on the end. No one was left as a wallflower because the hostess made sure that she introduced as many young men to as many girls as were necessary to fill the girls' and boys' programme cards. The young men fetched the girls from their chaperones and returned them to their seats after the dance. It was not good manners to book too many dances with the same girl as that would mean the plainer, less interesting girls would not have their cards filled in.

As we grew up, Mother would occasionally come and have a meal with us in the nursery and would critically watch our table manners. 'Do not make such a noise when you are eating, eat more slowly, take your elbows off the table, do not drink with food in your mouth; if you have to speak with food in your mouth, be sure to push it into your cheek and do not open your mouth too wide . . .'

During the First World War our home in Ireland became a hive of activity. Mother trained as a Red Cross nurse, and her sister Vera, wife of Stanley Tomkins, the former Governor of Uganda who had volunteered again for service, came over from England to live with us. The drawing-room became the room where all the action took place, such as rolling bandages and teaching first aid to young recruits of the Red Cross.

My mother started breeding Belgian hares for food and became the editor of the *Rabbit Keepers' Journal.* She wrote endless articles on how to keep rabbits for food and we all, however young, helped put the wrappers round the monthly magazine that went out to thousands of subscribers.

During the war, the Canadian army horses, their officers and grooms who had been billetted on us provided the greatest excitement for me. Amongst the officers was Mother's brother, Michael Masterman, who ran a ranch in Canada and adored horses. He loved my obvious enjoyment of them and carried me on the front of the saddle of his charger whenever he had time to spare. I was always to be found in the park amongst the legs of these great horses, whenever I managed to escape from Nanny's watchful eye. The gentle way they took sugar or carrots from me with their lips almost kissing my fingers made it quite clear that they would not hurt me. Eventually, the officers and their horses were all sent overseas on active service. Sadly, Uncle Michael was killed within weeks of being sent out, which upset my mother terribly. She built a library at St Columba's in his memory and called it the Masterman Library.

Holidays every summer were great fun when we were young. A month used to be booked in a hotel by the sea and we would go to places like Bundoran. The entourage was quite large. My father had a Cadillac, my mother a Model T Ford. The whole family went including Willie of course, the nursery maid, Nanny, and Jim, the Pomeranian. We could not take Sandy as he was too big. Father drove the Cadillac, the chauffeur Mother's Model T Ford.

There was a sort of pecking order as far as luggage was concerned. Mother and Father had huge brown trunks with a thick leather strap around them. As children, we had two trunks filled with every possible garment: combinations with long legs, woollen bands to go around our tummies, bathing suits made of alpaca which tied below the knees and up around the neck, and bathing caps which looked like pudding bowls made of green transparent waterproof material with elastic in them under which we stuffed our hair. It always amazed me that we were practically never uncovered on the beach, except for the brief period at sea. Our frilly dresses and hats were inevitably worn on the sojourns on the beach. In those days when one went bathing one did it from a bathing box drawn down to the sea edge. Mother taught us to wet our foreheads before dipping in to the sea, but what this was supposed to do, I don't know. We never plunged in as we would today, but held the skirt of our bathing suit and bobbed up and down. Eventually, with tremendous bravado, we dipped right up to our necks. Mother or Father held us under the chin with one hand, grabbed a large piece of bathing suit between our

At the seaside with our inevitable hats

shoulders and taught us to swim by slowly loosening the hold on our suits. I took to swimming like a duck takes to water. The sea held no fear for me. In fact when I was four I remember once it was very rough, a huge wave was coming at us and, in his hurry to get out of the sea, Charlie gave me a shove to start himself off. The wave knocked me down and Nanny had to rush into the sea, fully clothed, to pull me out. She then had to be taken back to the hotel to change her soaking clothes. I was not at all frightened by the adventure.

I will never forget one August when we came to England for our holiday and went to the Lake District. Mother's Model T Ford would not go up the steep gradients and she had to back it up one hill as the reverse gear gave more power than the forward one! She never had another car after the Ford as she could not face the 'new fangled' gear-boxes. Motoring in

Dressed in the new outfits Nanny had made for us

those days was quite an adventure, especially in the first car we had. It took a considerable time, for example, to get the hood up if it rained. Any undue exertion on the car's part up a steep hill made the engine boil. The sharp flint roads were forever puncturing the tyres. The dust made it necessary to wear hats with veils which completely covered our faces, and we had to shake our coats like a dog to get rid of our dust. We were covered up with enormous blue-lined fur rugs and the perennial picnic basket was full of hot refreshments and a thermos for the times we were sitting by the side of the road whilst the necessary repairs were done to the car. I do not remember a journey without these incidents. That was all part of the fun of holidays.

We were never without food of some sort and Nanny's canvas bag, which she seldom seemed to be without, always contained large packets of biscuits. We had waterproof knickers which we put on for paddling, in bright yellow water-proof material which pricked, plus all the buckets, the spades, the bathing suits, bathing caps and towels. I think Nanny and the nursery maid were more like beasts of burden than people. My greatest joy were the donkey rides on the beach. I was always to be found with the donkeys, even though we could not afford all the rides I would have wished for.

We only went away once a year, in August. Easter holidays were very much a religious celebration. Nanny made us all new outfits and I remember one in particular when we three girls had scarlet coats with black imitation fur collars and cuffs and bonnets to match and we went to the morning church service very proud of our new outfits. We usually spent the rest of the day at Easter time looking for wild violets and primroses.

Christmas was a tremendous celebration with an enormous Christmas tree in the college front hall and we drew and painted all our own Christmas cards. I cannot feel that the recipients of my efforts were very thrilled with them!

Schooldays

After the era of governesses, Charlie and Willie joined the boys in the school where my father taught, for their lessons, and eventually, Dene and I joined them too. I do not talk much about my father as I knew him so little. To me he was a tall, rather fierce man with a moustache which pricked if he kissed me, someone who whacked my brother with a cane when he refused to take off his cap to a woman friend of my mother's whom we all loathed, someone who removed me quickly and firmly from the classroom when I was innocently passing a crib from the boy next door to me to the one on my other side. I was the victim caught holding the crib when my father saw me, and the disgrace of being frog-marched from the classroom will remain with me for ever. I do not know what happened to the boys; a beating I expect for the cane was not spared at St Columba's in those days.

I wonder how much influence most fathers have on their daughters? Mine made me think that men were creatures to be well-respected. My first love affair occurred when I was six. A party was being given on the headmaster's tennis lawn for twenty of the older boys to celebrate my father's birthday;

OPPOSITE *Growing up*

strawberries and cream were the great treat. I sat next door to a very handsome fair-haired boy with whom I fell in love at first sight. As a mark of my admiration, I gave him my strawberries which he received with cool gratitude but his interest in me went no further than that. For years I loved this handsome boy in a girlish dream-like way. His name was Dermot Boyle. Then forty years later, a Lady Boyle rang me about the training of her Poodle. We got talking about Ireland and when she discovered I was the daughter of the late headmaster of St Columba's College, she said her husband had been to school there. She was the wife of my first love! However, it was not until many years later when I attended the prize-giving at my son's school, that there to give away the prizes was Air-Vice Marshall Sir Dermot Boyle, the schoolboy I had fallen in love with when I was six. I still think that I had very good taste for one so young! Patrick Campbell was another pupil at St Columba's College.

Readers must think I am always referring to what my parents told me in my young days. Perhaps I am strange in this present day world of despised parents to have modelled my life so much on what I was taught, but I firmly believe that experience is one of the most important things in life, and that anything my parents told me was right because they had had experience. This brings me to the fact that my father always insisted that we must never run up bills. If you wanted something you had to have the money to pay for it, or it was dishonest. What modern people would think of this advice, I do not know with all their credit systems and hire purchase; but it has always given me an inner peace to know that, with the exception of the telephone bill, I owe nobody anything. I utterly refuse to run up accounts. If I did, it would make the balance in my current account look bigger than it should be, and that gives one a false sense of well-being, stunts one's enterprise, and according to my father, makes one dishonest by living off other people's money. It is now obvious to me that one cannot make money with nothing behind one. All businesses are built up on credit, yet my conscience still says 'you cannot buy what you have not got the money to pay for'. Heaven knows which is right!

In my childhood days we were given only one penny a week. If we needed more than one penny a week, we could go to Mother and ask if there was any job to do whereby we could earn some money. She never refused to find us something to do, but it was not something easy. It made us realize the value of money, that extra one penny had to be gained by real effort or we did not get it. Ordinary things like cleaning the house or silver, were part and parcel of our normal existence, and only the boys in the family escaped it. This I never understood. Mother even cleaned my youngest brother's shoes for him. Many was the time that I remonstrated with her and suggested he was made to do this menial task for himself, but men in my mother's mind were creatures to be waited on hand and foot by their women folk. My eldest brother did not agree, and he certainly did his share of heavier household tasks when we lived at Oxford after my father had died, and our fleet of servants were things of the past. In my own household these things do not occur. I see nothing menial or unsuitable for men in the job of washing up, or even making beds.

My father had been a double blue in cricket and football at Oxford and played these games with the boys at St Columba's. One night, when I was nine years old, he died of a heart attack although he had been playing football that afternoon, and Mother was left a widow with four children and another on the way. Willie had to return to his parents in Dublin and, with little sympathy from the school authorities, we had to leave Ireland as the house was required for another headmaster. Father had owned a house called Sandfield at Headington, four miles from Oxford but, at that time, it was occupied by the Rowells who owned a jewellers in Oxford and they had to be given a year's notice to leave, so we went to Brighton for a year, to a dull house in a row with no place for animals. It was a dreary uneventful year so I will pass over it.

My brother, Desmond, was born in Brighton and Mother seemed completely besotted with him and used to say he was all she had left of Father. This, in my opinion, spoilt Desmond or Bobby, as we called him after the title of a favourite book about a very naughty boy. Bobby was rather fat from being fed on masses of Glaxo and he looked like the boy on the cover of that book. It was at that time, when I was about thirteen years old, that I wrote a long and illiterate poem on my hatred of babies. Bobby was a terrible screamer and at nights he kept us awake crying. All the baby foods in the world did not seem to suit him, so one night I asked if he could sleep in my room with his cot next to my bed, and when he cried, I used to pat him and say 'Thunder' in a very loud voice. This had the required effect, Bobby slept. Recently, I saw a television programme which said the best thing to make children go to sleep was noise, so perhaps I was ahead of my time. Bobby had seemingly non-caring nursery maids for throughout his early toddling days they all, with one exception, let him fall down the stairs. I cannot think how many times Bobby fell down the stairs without seriously hurting himself. The 'bump, bump' we heard so often, will always remain in my memory. Why no one put a gate at the top I cannot think, or if they did, why was it not kept shut? One day I had to take him out with me on the bus to Oxford. His face was all bruises, and the terrible remarks from the other passengers made me feel very miserable. It all added up to the fact that I hated babies. Yet in years to come when I had my own, I doubt if any mother could have loved them more. Even though I had a nanny, ninety per cent of the seeing after them was done by myself, which made the nannies feel useless and they left one by one. In the end, my own old nanny returned to me and took over and was not jealous of my wanting to care for my own children. Nanny lived to the age of ninety-eight, so it is obvious that hard work pays if you want to live a long life!

My change of heart towards children shows that one should never make up one's mind without leaving a loophole to alter one's opinion. The thing that always amazed me was that other people's children, when I was a youngster, did not recognize the fact that I was not over-keen on playing with them,

Sitting with Nanny, who returned to help me bring up my own children

and that I much preferred animals or sports of some kind. If I lay on the beach during our annual summer holiday in Cornwall, before long I would be surrounded by children. Sticky hands would go into mine, requests of 'please play with us' would drag me to my feet, and before I knew where I was, I, the 'baby-hater', would be the play mother to dozens of kids. Is it that the human child has little or no telepathy, that its trusting mind sees someone who may look fun, and in its own conceit decides to make that person like it willy-nilly? I believe that to be true, or maybe it was that they knew the real me, who when I became grown up, loved my children almost too much and certainly love other people's children too. I even taught for a short time in a kindergarten and I really enjoyed making up fairy stories to tell to wide-eyed youngsters, who believed every word, because I think I used an exciting tone of voice when recounting the made-up spontaneous tales. Today, I have no youngsters to tell fairy tales to, but I use the same tone of voice with dogs who believe that this voice means exciting hunts in the woods, or work in a film, or just lovely 'din dins'. Without my early experiences with small children, I would definitely never have realized what tone of voice can do to bring out the best, or even the worst, in both the animal and human kingdom. To this day, if I work in a film with a child, I can get it to do things quite happily that the director or its mother have been unable to get it to do. When Judith had her little girl, Harriet, she was ill after the birth and I took the baby home for a month. I was in my element and sent her back to her mother 'house-trained' and I hope, happy. I certainly felt like a mother again, rather than a grandmother.

Our holidays, when we were teenagers, were always great fun. Although we were desperately poor – Mother had only been left three hundred pounds a year to keep the house and family together – she always managed to save enough to take us to the sea, as of old, for the month of August and we usually took two or three other children from friends' families with us so that if we went to dances or anything, we had the right number of boys and girls. Everyone in our family played musical instruments, I played the piano and Hawaiian guitar, Charlie played the banjulele, Dene the mandoline, Mother the Spanish guitar and Bobby the percussion instruments so we had lovely sing-songs after our days by the sea and our excursions. Our dogs, Andy the Alsatian and Vanity the Fox Terrier, always came with us. We usually had a charming landlady in the house we rented so holidays were very enjoyable.

We always went to all the regattas that took place in Cornwall in those days. As I was, by that time, a first-rate swimmer and fairly good at diving, I entered all the races and won quite a nice lot of pocket money. I remember once during a race of

OPPOSITE *(Left to right) Charlie, Bobby, Dene,*
myself and Hazel at Sandfield

about one hundred yards, I was leading when the girl behind me threw up her arms and shouted for help. I went back to her and she immediately started to swim like mad in an effort to win the race! I realized what a dirty trick she had tried to play on me and was spurred on to make an even greater effort than hers and just managed to beat her. I vowed someone else could rescue the next person who tried this trick on me!

When we moved to Headington after Brighton, I went to a newly opened school called Headington School for Girls, a few hundred yards down the road from our home. There were only twelve girls there when Dene, Hazel and I started. One had to have an impeccable pedigree to gain admittance and we were definitely at a disadvantage since, owing to the very little money my mother had been left, we could not afford to wear clean blouses every day, or to have blazers bought for us like the other girls. As a result we were very much looked down on by some of the other girls and a few of the mistresses. The headmistress was terrifying. Her hair was cut like a man's and she would descend on us at great speed with her flowing gown if she happened to catch us doing something wrong, such as walking on the grass. I was frightened of her and she certainly did not class me as one of her favourite pupils. At this time, I had an old pony called Tommy and I spent all my spare time with him rather than doing my prep as I should have been doing. Not only did I come to school probably smelling of the stable but my mind would wander to Tommy instead of concentrating on the subject I was supposed to be taking in. My reports were always the same, 'Barbara will only work if the subject interests her', and with the exception of geography and botany, the subjects did not interest me. Well, surely it was the duty of the teacher to make the subjects interest me; it was their failure not mine, which showed up clearly when, in later years I went to college and gained very

OPPOSITE ABOVE *Our new home, Sandfield*
BELOW *Walking around Headington, collecting for the RSPCA*

high marks in all the exams. Why? Because the subjects were put over in an interesting way and I was not treated as a sub-standard object.

I feel this in the training of dogs. People are forever telling me that their dogs are impossible. Their dogs are not impossible, it is the owners who are difficult. If the dogs are interested in the work they are being taught, they carry out the exercises with gaiety and pleasure, and give deep adoration to the teacher. If the owners are drab or do not believe their dogs are good, they lose the rapport with their dogs and achieve nothing. Praise and admiration are the greatest beautifiers; that is why people in love have such a radiance, they are being uplifted by beautiful thoughts and words. I often think, had I received a little praise at school, instead of perpetual scolding, I might have done some good. I left school at the age of sixteen, heartily glad to say good-bye to my days there. Some years later I was most surprised to be asked to donate one pound for the provision of a chair with my name on so I suppose the existence of my name, along with hundreds of others on the chairs in the Assembly Hall, will remind people that I did at one time have some sort of education!

At the age of fourteen, before I left school I secretly entered myself for the Harper Adams Agricultural College without my mother's knowledge. However, when I left school, they could not take me for another twelve months so my grandmother generously offered to pay for me to go to a finishing school in Switzerland for a year. My grandmother was a funny mixture of love and haughty dominance. She lived in a hotel in Paris in the Champs-Élysées, after losing her home and belongings to the Russian revolutionaries and after the death of her husband. She still had, however, a very large personal income which she lavished almost entirely on destitute princes from the Russian revolution. She bought them taxis so that they could earn their living in Paris. They all adored her, though whether it was cupboard love we shall never know. They were at her beck and call wherever she went. Even when she met me at the Metropole Hotel in London, a prince was hovering in the

(Left to right) Dene, myself, Hazel and Bobby at Sandfield

background, waiting for my departure. Actually this was my first and only meeting with her. It took place there when I was thirteen years old and it was a devastating experience. I went at her invitation to lunch. We sat down to eat when she took one look at me and exclaimed 'You are hideous'. She then gave me half a crown and told me to go to the zoo – I am sure she felt the hovering prince could not meet such an ugly child! In fact I already knew that I was ugly for I had once overheard my mother saying to Nanny, 'Why can't Barbara be pretty like Dene and Hazel?' I was not meant to have heard this but I think that is the reason I turned all my love to animals. They did not care what I looked like.

My grandmother never wanted to be called by the name Granny so we all had to call her 'Myth', goodness knows why! I do not like my own grandchildren to call me Granny or Grandmother so I ask them to call me 'Granmummy' which I like.

*Dene with the kiss-curl
that was 'in' then*

*Hazel in her teens
with one of the few
Alsatians in England
at that time, which
we bred*

After Myth had offered to send me to Switzerland, we obtained a lot of brochures from Truman and Knightley, the scholastic agents, and studied them carefully. The brochure that sounded most attractive was the one giving details of a school in Lausanne, Switzerland, which was owned by three sisters. It promised a first-class finishing school education in languages (which I loved), winter sports, riding and much else.

Before going there for my first term, my Aunt Claire from Scarborough had offered to send me on a winter sports holiday with the CSSM (the Children's Special Service Mission) which apparently specialized in taking three hundred girls and three hundred boys skiing, adding as a bonus religious instruction. Only well brought up children seem to have been accepted and the boys were strictly segregated from the girls in different hotels and were forbidden to meet the girls during the winter sports activities. Unfortunately, on the long train journey, I met a boy from Eton, Robert Raphael, and fell hopelessly in love with him. Rules about segregation were ignored and I went skiing with him on the glorious slopes of Engleberg. I had never skied before and was in my seventh heaven when he taught me. As bad luck would have it, a photographer, one of the many who take photographs and put them in the local shop hoping for sales, took a photograph of Robert and I on the slopes, and who should see it, but a housemother in charge of us girls. I was commanded that evening to go to her room where a sort of tribunal of housemothers and an older girl greeted me; it seemed almost like a court. They asked me why I had disobeyed the rules and threatened that, unless I promised not to do it again, I would not be allowed out by myself. They even asked me whether I knew Jesus, and was I saved? It staggered me that I, who had two brothers and had been brought up in a boys' public school, should have been considered a sinner for having harmlessly skied with a very nice young boy of about seventeen, my own age. I replied that my father was a clergyman and our Christian upbringing had been very strict, that I saw no harm in what I had done and I am afraid I went on meeting Robert. Alas, the holiday came to an end. He went on to Chillon College while I went to my finishing school and a term of absolute hell.

The school had a lovely view of the valley and Lake Leman. There were twenty-six girls, two Swiss teachers and a newly arrived English teacher. We were made to work very hard, having French crammed into us all day long, from 6.30 a.m. to 9 p.m., with the exception of meal times, and with one hour's break in the afternoon when we went for a walk in a crocodile. We were utterly starved and my weight went down from ten stone to six-and-a-half stone, then I became ill. My face and neck swelled so that you could not tell my shoulders from my face and nobody seemed to know what was wrong. I was kept in my bedroom. Nobody came near me and no food was given to me except for two glasses of milk a day because the swelling caused my jaws to be clamped together. I managed to get a girl to post a letter to my mother, who did not realize from my description of my illness that I had mumps, and she got in touch with my grandmother in Paris. Myth asked her doctor to come to Lausanne and see me. He duly arrived, opened the door, exclaimed, *'Mon Dieu, les oreillons!'* and fled, worried about what his patients in his fashionable practice would do if he caught the mumps. After about three weeks, my swelling went down and I was allowed out of my prison. I had tried to write to Robert at Chillon but he never answered. When I was well, he invited me out with his mother who had come from England to see him and we had tea in Lausanne, the first good meal I had had for weeks.

Our letters home telling our parents how unhappy we were never seemed to arrive. We never went to winter sports and the nearest we got to fulfillment of the promise of sport was skating on the local reservoir with the Swiss teacher. She could not skate herself and we cruelly left her in the middle of the lake struggling to get to the edge. She was not a bad old thing, so eventually, someone went and helped her skate back to the bank. We did go riding once a week. This was the only time I was happy as I was always given the friskiest horse with which I had a great rapport.

One girl at the school had a nervous breakdown and could not stop reading her French Bible. All day long, she talked French to herself until we wondered what we should do for her. One German girl with great initiative got her family to send her large hampers of food which she sat up half the night eating all by herself. I plotted to run away. On Sundays we were all taken to Lausanne Cathedral for the mid-morning service and I reckoned the best thing to do was to get off the tram on the opposite side to all the others when it stopped and bolt for it. I did this and got a train to the frontier. Unfortunately, I had forgotten the Mesdames had my passport. They had notified the police that I had run away and I was taken back to the school rather ignominiously, shut in my room and nicknamed *'La Sauvage'*. I only mixed with the rest of the pupils during lessons and then was ordered back to my room to stay alone as punishment. From my window one day, I saw the three old Mesdames go out so I went to their study and asked the telephone operator for the English Consulate. I spoke to the Consul and described the conditions at this *pensionnat*. He sent up one of his staff who, on speaking to the English mistress and seeing how ill I was, arranged for all the students to be escorted back to London by a member of the consular staff. It took me some months to fully regain my health after this.

Happy days at college

The months soon flew by and the day approached when I was to go to Harper Adams Agricultural College. I was the only girl on the Agricultural side although there were girls in the Poultry Husbandry Institute a short distance away. I lived with them at the Ancellor Hostel and shared my room with a girl called Vera Ashmole, a descendant of the man who had founded the Ashmolean Museum at Oxford. We became devoted friends and I still correspond with her even after all these years. We used to write our diaries every evening in verse. Unfortunately when I later went to the Argentine, my mother threw away all my college things, including my diaries which I was very annoyed about as those were the happiest of days.

In those days, a girl at an agricultural college taking subjects like building construction and surveying, veterinary science and engineering, was almost unheard of, but I revelled in it. I was with animals all day long, learning as much as I could about everything to do not only with animal husbandry but also with the growing and harvesting of crops, book-keeping, the making of butter and cheeses and the care of fruit

OPPOSITE *Outside Harper Adams Agricultural College*

45

trees. It was a very comprehensive syllabus and I loved every minute. In the evenings there were entertainments galore. I took the leading lady's part in the college plays. I entered and won shooting and bridge competitions at college. Later, when I left, I played county tennis and hockey and also won the annual car rally in my 1923 bullnosed Morris against which much more modern cars competed, Vera acted as navigator. I managed to get the second highest marks of all the students by being praised instead of being cursed, figuratively speaking, as I had been at school. I was even trained at college in the secrets of the four-cylinder engine and, thanks to my sensitive fingers and keen ear, I have always been able to tune the engines of all our cars.

I have a very keen ear for anything that is wrong with a car and used to offer my services to the local motor company to run their new cars around the block and tell them what was wrong with them so that the customer pre-delivery service would be more efficient. I could not believe that their business would not increase enormously if they sent out cars that did not spend their first 2,000 or 3,000 miles on the road going back for repairs, which I am sorry to say is what happens with most cars today. However, the answer to my suggestion was 'Oh, no thank you, we would never make any profit if we put right all the things you would find were wrong', which is a sad reflection on the motor manufacturers. I have spent a vast number of hours of my time arguing with these manufacturers. I do not see why, when I buy a new car, I should have perpetual trouble. I fail to see why I should believe the customer relation chappies when they say that my car is 'standard' with all the faults I find in it, and I utterly fail to see why the cars should not be made to stand up to their guarantee which is part and parcel of the deal. You would imagine when these engineers are sent from the factory to try out one's car, that they would

OPPOSITE *The hockey and tennis teams at college; I played tennis a few times for Shropshire and hockey for Cheshire*

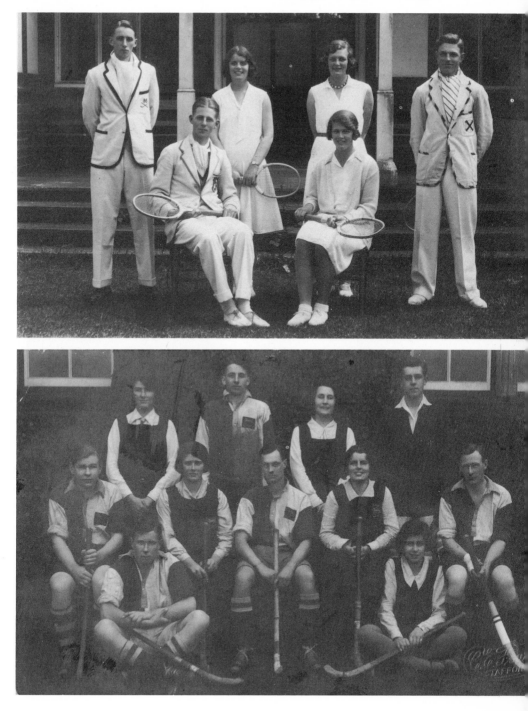

At a car rally which I won
against more modern cars in
my 1923 Morris. Did the number
plate predict my future name?

. . . and later outside my
Wolseley Daytona

realize they were not talking to someone who did not know a
big end from a baby's bottom, and that the word 'standard'
must be a red rag to a bull when there can be no such thing as
standard. I will give you a perfect example of this. I once
bought a new car which gave me trouble from the day it came.
I have never had to fight so many battles as I did with the
garage or the works customer relations department to get
everything wrong put right. In the end they agreed to do
something they very seldom or, according to them, never did;
take the car back into the works and put it right. For the three
weeks they had it I insisted they lent me a works car. This they
did; a much older one than mine and a much cheaper model.
Never have I enjoyed driving anything so much. She never
gave me a day's bad motoring, she was fast, silent, easy to

handle and cheap on consumption of petrol. When they said my own car was ready, I suggested they gave me one hundred pounds back and let me keep the two-year-old car instead of my brand new one. This they would not agree to; all they would offer me was to take my new car in equal exchange for their old one, which I would have been crazy to accept. I never got the new one to my satisfaction and sold it when it had under 3,000 miles on the clock. This company has lost my custom. I expect they said 'good riddance' when I was out of earshot, but I wonder really whether this type of incident does the car industry any good. I am constantly told that I am an exceptional person, that the average driver knows nothing about cars and that, to hide the noises, they put on the wireless and drive the car until its collapse seems imminent. I try to explain that I love cars, that I have rallied them, that I have learnt a lot about their insides and treat them with loving care. I hate to hear an engine running roughly. I cannot bear squeaks and rattles, or a gear-box that resists the gear change. I should hate to have an automatic change, it would deprive me of one of the greatest joys of a good car, a faultless gear change at any speed. The tuning of a car so that, even at quite high speeds it gives a good petrol consumption, is something that is possible with nearly all makes and to achieve this, one has to spend hours getting everything just right. I have often seen surprised motorists stare at me when I am looking under the bonnet, wondering if they should stop and offer assistance to the poor woman in distress, but running a car and tuning it on the road is the only way, I believe, to get the best out of it. I remember once a factory engineer came and tested a car of mine whose gear-box I complained was falling to bits. He tested it and said it was perfectly all right, thirty miles later and twelve hours after his test, all the tabs fell off and we had to install a new gear-box. I bet his company were pleased with him!

After carrying out experimental work for the Ministry of Agriculture, I left the college for good and have only been back once, long after I had married. The only memory anyone will

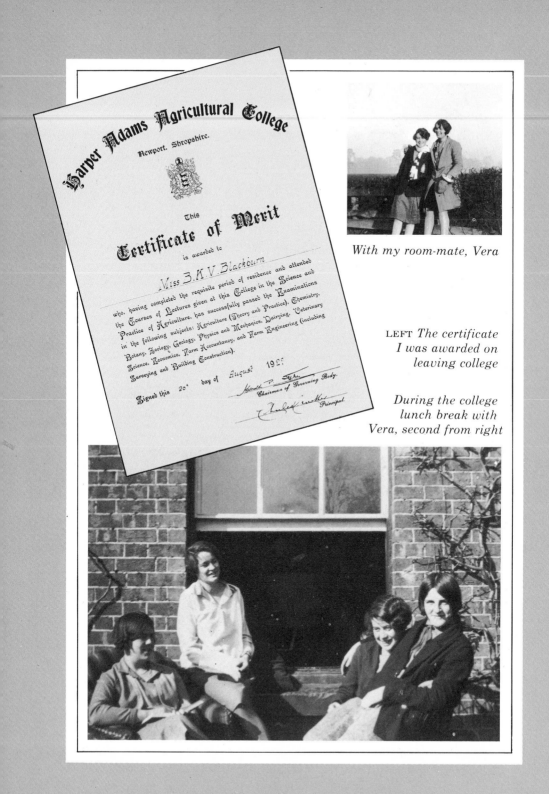

Harper Adams Agricultural College

Newport, Shropshire.

This

Certificate of Merit

is awarded to

Miss B.K.V. Blackburn

who, having completed the requisite period of residence and attended the Courses of Lectures given at this College in the Science and Practice of Agriculture, has successfully passed the Examinations in the following subjects: Agriculture (Theory and Practice), Chemistry, Botany, Zoology, Geology, Physics and Mechanics, Dairying, Veterinary Science, Economics, Farm Accountancy, and Farm Engineering (including Surveying and Building Construction).

Signed this 20ᵗ day of August 19⊃⊃

Chairman of Governing Body.

Principal

With my room-mate, Vera

LEFT *The certificate I was awarded on leaving college*

During the college lunch break with Vera, second from right have of me is the photograph in the Entrance Hall of all the students in 1928 which shows me amongst a sea of men.

College days were as happy as any young person could wish. The men treated me like gold and I had their respect. I remembered my mother's teachings so that, although I had lots of flirtations, nothing really very serious came out of them whilst at college. Mother had always said that love should be treated like porcelain china, taking the greatest care not to harm anyone or break their hearts. Love is something that can make or mar one's whole existence. She insisted that we never led any young men up the garden path. Men get their passions so easily aroused, she would say, that it is unfair on the girls' part to encourage them and then leave them cold. If men admire or love one this affection must always be treated with the greatest kindness and, even if it leads nowhere, they should remain friends. The 'chucking' of boy friends was something that only occurred in the servants hall. This may sound very old-fashioned today, but to me it is good advice. These days young people change their boy or girl friends like their underclothes, with little feeling for the broken or cracked hearts they leave behind. Friendship hardly seems to exist. Love, often in its crudest form, seems to be galloped into headlong without paving the way with friendship first, and without finding out whether true companionship is not an essential of true love long before sex comes into it. This attitude, I am sure, has been aggravated and encouraged by television and newspapers which only bring up the sex side of two young people's lives. Nobody ever told me anything about sex. I knew from animals roughly what went on in the human race, and I was not curious to find out any more until I had married the man I loved. Men must have found me peculiar in that I did not wish to be kissed by every young man who brought me home after a dance, and if any man did kiss me on my doorstep with more passion than should be shown except in the privacy of one's marriage bedroom, he was 'out' there and then. I kept my kisses for the people I had affection for. At college on the agricultural side, I was the only girl amongst

A Saturday afternoon outing with some of my men friends – fellow students at Harper Adams College

sixty men. Had I been too easy with my affections life would have been less fun, as, between the ages of sixteen and twenty, young men are at their most amorous. I loved every minute of life at college. I spent most evenings walking the countryside with one or another of the students there. We learned about life in a nice way; I had lots of mild love affairs, lots of proposals of marriage, even one from a member of the staff who had never been closer to me than behind a desk, but he proposed to me in a wonderful letter, saying he wanted me as his wife because I was always laughing. I can think of more sensible ways of choosing a wife, but I was deeply honoured, and I hope, wrote him a kind refusal. I think perhaps my rather old-fashioned treatment of men's advances intrigued them. They used to propose to me with letters accompanied by huge bouquets of flowers or extravagant boxes of chocolates and my sister would giggle over the letters, while I would feel sad for these men, so obviously unsuited to being my mate. Usually the weaker types were those most strongly attracted to me and my way of life. I would have been a sort of life insurance to them, I suppose, carrying their burdens and smoothing their way, yet they were not my ideals at all. I loved good looks and tallness. I had always had beautiful animals and I certainly wanted a good-looking husband, but it was kindness and gentleness and the love of animals that I looked for, or rather hoped for, because I never looked for men, they were just beings that entered my very busy life and gave me infinite pleasure in their company. I corresponded for over twenty-five years, long after I was married, with lots of my former young men. Some were stopped from writing to me when they themselves married and their wives were jealous; why, I cannot imagine. Could they not see that had I wanted their husbands, I could have had them long before they came on the scene? But then I do not understand some women. Men and women have a lot to give each other, even in correspondence; you do not have to love or want each other for yourself, but simply need

John Sainsbury, nicknamed 'Sausage' at college, plays the fool

53

with love & best
wishes from "Alden"
& Barbara.

to share ideas and friendship – but then I do not have a dirty mind so to me, there is no harm in friendship. I have had wonderful men friends, wonderful girl friends and only life's business has kept me from seeing more of all of them. But when one is up to one's eyes in work and rearing a family, there is little time left for friends. Yet if I do, by chance, meet someone I knew fifty years ago I can pick up the threads just where we dropped them that long time ago. I am always thrilled to meet old friends and acquaintances. People whose dogs I have trained many years ago, suddenly turn up with a new generation of dogs to be trained, and it makes me terribly happy to meet them again. Suddenly, through a woman's magazine article about me, I started to correspond with the girl who had lived next door in Ireland and whom I had not seen or heard of for fifty years. It gave me enormous pleasure to meet her again by letter after all this time. Another one from South Africa also got in touch with me through articles of mine in the same magazine and recalled incidents of thirty years ago when she lived for a time in my mother's house. Again, reminiscing was the greatest fun. It is a pity that so many nice people pass out of one's life. At my age so many will never come back; the past is fun to bring back to mind, the future always does not seem so bright. They say as one grows old that one's memory goes back farther and farther; if you meet people to reminisce with this can be proved or disproved.

OPPOSITE *On Alder, one of the ponies from the riding school I ran after leaving college*

Marriage and early war years

After I left college, I did various things like running a riding school, temporarily being a companion to an aunt and eventually going to the Argentine, all of which I have written about in my book, *Talking to Animals,* so I will not repeat it here.

On my return to England, I horse-dealt and it was through a former undergraduate friend of mine, Dr Felix Ingham, whom I knew before I went to the Argentine, that I met my husband, in a pub! As neither of us drink, it was an unusual place for us to meet. Felix, having heard that I had some horses again, used to turn up at Sandfield and help me exercise them. It was purely a platonic friendship. One evening, he suggested we meet at the George public house and then go on to Bampton Fair, some distance away. I was there at six o'clock, the appointed time and he was late so I said to the barmaid, 'Tell Dr Ingham that I wait for no man' and was actually going out of the door when he and another doctor, whom he introduced as Michael Woodhouse, came in and we all went to Bampton Fair. Few will believe me when I tell them that love at first sight is definitely possible. I fell head over heels in love with Michael.

OPPOSITE *My wedding day*

57

Just Barbara

I was at that time running dances on Saturday evenings at Sandfield and inviting all my girl friends to meet the young doctors from the Radcliffe Infirmary. Michael came to the next one and I am afraid, instead of being a good hostess and introducing everyone to each other as usual, I was out in the garden with Michael. Every evening we strolled by the river and the weather that summer stayed gloriously hot and dry for a very long time. Rumours of war brought us even closer together in the fear that, if war broke out, we might be separated. Six weeks after meeting we were engaged, much to the apparent annoyance of the other young doctors who could see their Saturday evening dances dwindling into nothing. One remarked, 'Engaged to Michael. Who is going to run the dances now?' As the phoney war broke out, I took a job as a sort of personal assistant, secretary/help to one of the consultants at the Radcliffe and saw Michael quite often as he was in the gynaecological department under Professor Stalworthy and I was quite close by. We married the following August and our wedding must have been one of the most extraordinary ones ever.

As I was dressing to go the church where my brother was to give me away, I suddenly got the most terrible cramp in my stomach. I could not stand up at all. Mother hastily telephoned Michael at the hospital and he came up and gave me some morphia which temporarily stopped the pain but made my mouth so dry I could hardly speak. Charlie, my brother, had to go to church with a small bottle of water under his coat with which to wet my lips should I not be able to speak very easily. The service went off all right but the pain started to return after we got back for the reception, so we told our guests that we had to get away on our honeymoon, quickly changed, got into the car and drove just around the corner where we stayed until we thought everyone had gone away. I was in agony by then so we went back to Sandfield and I went to bed. Three days later we started our honeymoon in the Speech House Hotel in Gloucestershire; the bombs could be heard falling at infrequent intervals in the background.

Another honeymoon couple were staying in the hotel and we chatted with them the first evening. Next morning they came down to breakfast quarrelling viciously. The girl got up from the table, said she was leaving him forever, packed her bags and, I think, departed. We went out for a walk after a ghastly night spent in the room where King Henry VIII and one of his wives was said to have slept. In fact, we came to the conclusion that he and all six of his wives must have slept in the bed together. During the walk we stopped in a bracken glade and I sat on a bee and got badly stung. I am allergic to this sort of thing so we decided honeymoons were not for us and returned to Oxford. Shortly after this, Michael was called up but failed his medical as he had had pleural effusion of one lung. He therefore took over a practice in Melksham in Wiltshire from a young doctor who had been called up for the Navy.

I will pass over the years that followed as I have written about them elsewhere, and come to the time when, at last, we settled in a farm of our own in Croxley Green. My husband had then qualified for a post as Consultant in Physical Medicine at St Mary's Hospital, Paddington, where he stayed for twenty-six years until he retired.

OVERLEAF *On the farm with my cows*

ABOVE *Juno and Sixpence, the pony I bred at Melksham*
OPPOSITE *Juno helps around the farm*

By now, I was happy with my seventeen cows and my
half-bred Arab Welsh ponies and their foals. I started lecturing and going all over the country to women's luncheon clubs.
I did some television and radio shows, including the second
What's My Line that went out with Eamonn Andrews as chairman and Lady Barnett and Gilbert Harding on the panel. It
was great fun and they did not guess my occupation, which
was of course training dogs. My own dogs by this time had
become famous in films and television and the money they
earned built the house we now live in. We had previously lived
in the large house opposite where we had run the first ever
residential dog training courses. These were enormous fun.
People came from all over the country and we trained seventeen people and their dogs in three days. Formerly, I had run a

trial weekend dog training course at Dorian Williams' place, Pendley Manor in Tring. I had asked in the *Daily Mirror* for twenty-five of the worst dogs in Britain to come and promised I would train them in five days. Dogs of all sorts and sizes came, from a savage Alsatian to a tiny Griffon. All were trained to perfection in the time and I had a film made of the proceedings called *School for Problem Dogs.* I was so encouraged by the success of this venture that I shortened the time needed to train up to thirty-two dogs and owners to six-and-a-half hours. The pupils and their dogs stayed in local hotels and were always very welcome. The managers of the various hotels said you would never have known there were so many dogs in the hotel. Many of the pupils were show dogs, but most of them were just ordinary people's dogs. One owner, Charles Scott-Paton, came on eight courses and when he booked his last one, I said, 'Oh no, Charles, you cannot need another one' and he laughingly replied 'Don't flatter yourself, dear, it is the food I am coming for'. These pupils all stayed in the big Campions when we lived there, before we moved to our present house and took the name 'Campions' with us. It had sixteen rooms and the deep wall cupboards had been turned into indoor kennels for the dogs. I showed films in the evenings and was always very sad when we said goodbye

My visitors' book includes comments from a pupil who had come from India

Our original Campions

to our pupils on the Sunday afternoon. Charles Scott-Paton must have been unique with his pets; he had a white cockatoo which liked to be free but soiled his secretary's papers so he built a large cage in his office, put the secretary inside and let the cockatoo fly unfettered!

As my dog training ventures grew bigger and bigger, I was always being approached by different charities to do demonstrations of dog training or to take a number of dogs I had

OVERLEAF *One of the classes at my dog training residential school*

With Juno and Chica

trained to give a display of what they could do. I always
remember how, at one such show, I had decided to include our
little English Toy Terrier, Chica, who, although obedience
trained and a winner in the obedience ring, never really made
films or went on television as my Great Danes, Juno and later
Junia, had done. I decided to have a bag snatcher steal someone's handbag as she was, supposedly, walking in the park.
The thief snatched the bag and ran. I sent Juno, who was
trained in policework, after the thief and then I pretended she
had given up the chase and stopped her. Tiny Chica then went
after him, caught hold of his trousers and brought him to the
ground. The crowd simply loved it. It is easy to amuse a crowd

with obedience-trained dogs. We used flags in another demonstration. We would bring on several flags of different countries but, of course, only the British one had my scent as I had held it under my arm for a few minutes. We then asked Juno various questions, including which country did she belong to and in she would go and pick up the British flag.

One year I decided to run a 'Dog's Day' in aid of making a film for the Guide Dogs for the Blind called *Trouble with Junia,* which was recently shown on BBC television. This 'Dog's Day' was very easy to run. All we needed was a fairly big open space and trusses of straw around the arena for the crowd to watch from. We had games such as the 'thread the needle' race in which the competitors and their dogs stand at one end of the arena and an assistant holding a big-eyed darning needle stands at the other end. On the signal to go, the dogs and their owners run as fast as they can to the other end, the owners then have to thread the needle with the hand with which they are holding the dog on a lead. It is not as easy as you may think if the dog will not sit still or keep still. They do not run back with the needle, but the assistant just holds up his arm to show that the needle is threaded. There is also the 'potato' race in which the dog owner has to run and pick up

Showing a young pupil how to correct her dog at one of my demonstrations

each potato separately while holding the dog on a lead, put the potatoes one by one in a small bucket at the other end of the course and run with the bucket back to the starting line. Very often it is this last effort which brings them to grief. The 'egg and spoon' race is run in the same way with the spoon held in the hand that also holds the lead. The 'ball and bucket' race consists of four tiny rubber balls in a bucket of water. The owner with the dog runs up to the bucket and the dog has to fish out the tiny floating balls one by one and must drop them into another bucket. Only well-trained dogs can do this. Then we had the 'drop on command' race in which the owner and dog run to a white line. The dog has to drop into the down position and the owner runs on alone to another marker line whereupon, he turns and runs back to the finishing post, picking the dog up on the way. There are many more ideas for fun and *Nationwide* filmed the 'Dog's Day' we ran at Campions. This type of day encourages people to train their dogs and the dogs seem to enjoy the excitement. The 'three-legged' race with each of the competitors holding a dog lead in their hand, was the race that always got the most mix-ups and tumbles.

I always gave a demonstration of dog training in the interval when I would ask for any dog to be brought to me and demonstrated that, unless it was vicious or mentally deficient, it could do basic obedience in under six minutes. The trouble with doing this is that many people then say that the dog has already been trained beforehand which is something I always avoid as it is no fun if one cheats. I always remember the agents for the 'Dulux dogs' commercials phoning me one day and telling me that their publicity girl was buying an Old English Sheepdog in Somerset early that morning and bringing it to me for training at 11 a.m. Would I be able to train it and teach the girl to work it so that it could catch the 2 p.m. plane overseas to make a commercial? I did this with minutes to spare. I trained all the star 'Dulux dogs', including Digby,

OPPOSITE *Training a Dulux dog*

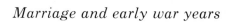

Duke meets one of his seven children

for filming. The latest one is Duke; the youngest one was six weeks old and did his first commercial at seven weeks. He had a fantastic brain and understanding; in three half-hour lessons he learned to sit and stay, walk up to the tin, jump on it and stand there, bark and jump off and go out of the frame. He also learned to jump up and scratch a wall. Unfortunately he only made one set of commercials as his owner died and he went back to the breeder.

The trouble with training dogs for filming is that they get so hot in the studio that they start panting and it is then very difficult to make them look asleep, when I am required to do so by the script. I find the Old English Sheepdog a very easy breed to train but very difficult to keep looking beautiful for filming. Their mouths turn a dirty brown from dribbling and they are forever being chalked and dried. If it rains during filming they have to go out in boots, with waterproofs on their back and tummy so that their coat stays dry and white.

My first series on dog training was done in the early fifties when I was the trainer in the BBC programme, *The Smokey Club,* a monthly Scottish television series and, most months, I had to go up to Glasgow or Edinburgh with Juno to do training. Then, much later on, I did a series of eight six-minute shows on *Pebble Mill at One.* I loved this as each week they brought me a dog with a different problem. I had also adopted a puppy, Bella, from the Birmingham lost dogs home for the programme and she appeared for a few seconds each week doing something more advanced each time. The trouble was that she and I got so attached to each other that she would scream with jealousy when I said 'what a good dog' to that week's problem dog! I think people must have thought she was being murdered. The series brought me thousands of letters from viewers who wanted the problems with their dogs solved and I was exhausted trying to answer them all. I have never had a secretary because I feel that, by the time I have dictated a letter and it has been typed and signed, I could have written direct myself. Even though I type back to front very often and make terrible spelling mistakes; I still think the message does get through. People so often forget to enclose a stamp with their queries that I keep telling myself that one day I will have to throw their letters ruthlessly away in the rubbish basket, though I have never done so yet!

Itinerary for Barbara Woodhouse in San Francisco

Wednesday, January 24

9:00 10:00 p.m. — Arrives S.F. - Will arrange for Driver to pick up
and take her to St. Francis Hotel

Thursday, January 25

6:45 a.m. — KGO-TV - "AM" Show - Jim Dunbar - "live" - *(Show has been prompted, tons for pictures)*
277 Golden Gate Avenue - (need 2 dogs)

8:45 a.m. — KYA Radio - Larry Brownell - taping - In Room

9:00 a.m. — S.F. Chronicle-Examiner - Eloise Dungan - In Room -
(Will bring photographer) (need dogs)

11:00 a.m. — KRON-TV News - Ray Taliaferro - taping - 1001 Van Ness
(need 1 or 2 dogs)

11:30 a.m. — KCBS-FM Radio - Mike Beeson - 1/2 hr. taping -
#1 Embarcadero Center

12 - Noon — KCBS-AM Radio News - Sharon Lovejoy - taping -
#1 Embarcadero Center

12:30 p.m. — KFRC Radio - (Will also be used on KFRC's FM station) -
Don De Fesi - 1/2 hr. taping - 415 Bush

1:30 p.m. — KSFX Radio - John Catchings - taping - 1177 Polk

2:00 p.m. — Eloise Keeler - Pet Editor - S.F. Chronicle-Examiner
Combo paper - Telephone Interview - Call 388-1896
from Room in St. Francis

2:15 p.m. — Darla Miller - San Jose Mercury-News - In Room at
St. Francis Hotel - (will bring photographer - Need 1 dog

Thursday, January 25

3:40 p.m. — KKHI Radio - Bill Hollenbeck - taping for "Book Corner"
show - St. Francis Hotel

4:00 - 5:00 p.m. — Joan MacKinney - Oakland Tribune - In Room -
(Will bring photographer) - (Need dogs)

5:00 - 6:30 p.m. — Group Interview Session - in Room at St. Francis -
(Would be nice to have dogs)
KUSF Radio - Steve Zimmerman
KPFA Radio - Margo Skinner
KSAY Radio - "Mick" Seeber

Friday, January 26

9:00 a.m. - 11:00 — KGO Radio - Jim Dunbar - "live" - telephone show -
277 Golden Gate

11:15 a.m. — Leave for Airport

12:00 - Noon — Leave for Chicago - American Airlines - Flt. 474 -
Arriving 5:45 p.m. - Will be taken to Airport

Please Note: KCRA-TV News was going to do an interview but we had to
cancel it because it was necessary for Barbara Woodhouse
to leave early for Chicago.

America

My husband and I had a wonderful time in 1973 when my books were all published in the United States by Stein and Day of New York who took us both over there on a promotion tour. We had never done anything like this before. We were told that there would not be time to collect our luggage from the aircrafts we would be travelling on most days, so everything we took had to be carried in hand luggage. Well, as we were going for four weeks, this seemed rather a tall order. We had two plastic bags which were the right size to fit under the seat in the plane and I bought crease-resistant clothes. We went in January, so I also bought a pair of long boots, lined with sheepskin, to keep me warm and soon found these an absolute menace since, by some freak of the weather, there was nearly a heat wave when we got to New York. I never wore the boots the whole time we were in the States. Our plastic bags, however were received with some misgivings by several of the bell boys at the smart hotels we stayed in, especially the Beverley Hills Hotel in Los Angeles.

Michael and I flew to New York where we were met by Stein and Day's publicity girl who took us to our hotel. Next

OPPOSITE *My two-day schedule*

morning, we began the most concentrated publicity tour that I could ever have thought possible. We started by doing CBS news at 6.45 in the morning, and by chance I mentioned that I had with me the addresses in America of the American servicemen whose dogs I had trained in England, and that it would be a particular joy to meet some of my former pupils – both animal and human! Perhaps, I suggested, it might be possible for one or two to come on a programme with me? We looked up one address, a Mr Jaffe of Philadelphia. He was there and still had the dog, a Cavalier King Charles, that I had trained for him. He was delighted to come with his dog for an early morning interview.

I was astonished to find how many appointments Stein and Day had arranged for me. I did as many as fourteen television, radio and press interviews in a day. We were rushed from one studio to another. I never knew what we were going to do next. One man, I remember, handed me a dog with the words, 'Be careful, it has just bitten the porter' but it was a lovely Komondor dog. I could not find anything wrong with it at all and gave it basic training in under six minutes: 'Walk to heel, sit, stay, down, stay, come.' Then, for a joke, I handed it to the interviewer, a rather nervous lady and said 'Now, you try and see what you can do.' It did everything for her as well; she was thrilled.

I was interviewed by a lot of newspapers. They had tape recorders and were all asking me questions at the same time. How they got anything on their machines I do not know, but I had the most wonderful press coverage. I went on all the major shows over most of the States, although unfortunately, I did not get to stay in the Deep South, but the welcome everywhere I went was unbelievable. One newspaperman, Walter Fletcher of the *New York Times,* interviewed me and said that they were not convinced that I could train a dog in six minutes and would like to do a test. So I said, of course, and asked him what test would they like me to do? Mr Fletcher then told me that he had two friends with dogs, one an Alsatian, the other a Lhasa Apso. The dogs were awful enemies and had never been able to meet since the first occasion when they had fought each other so savagely. How would I like to train these two in six minutes? I replied that I thought that would be absolutely lovely and asked him to bring the dogs to our hotel. The two dogs duly arrived at the St Moritz Hotel at a safe distance from each other. They had come up in separate lifts as they were such terrible fighters and would have killed each other. Even so, they could smell each other's scent and began to make such angry noises that one of the owners said she thought she had better go home. Eventually, I persuaded her to let me have a go at both of the dogs. I put choke chains on them and gave them each a really hard jerk, telling them to 'leave' when they started growling. I then taught them both basic obedience on the landing of the hotel and they were absolutely perfect from that time on. A few minutes later they were both sitting side by side on the sofa with me.

The next day, the article admitting that I could do it, was certainly most flattering. And so the publicity went on. No sooner had I arrived in one television studio, than a board would go up announcing that Barbara Woodhouse was wanted in Studio 2. All the different companies' studios seemed to be in the same building so that I could give five or six appearances a day without having to leave the building.

There was one thing that I thought was excellent. As you went into one of these big television blocks, there was always a board in the foyer which read 'Such and such a company welcomes Barbara Woodhouse' together with all the other names of the people who were going to appear in one or other of the company studios during that day. This all had the effect of making one feel very welcome. I have seldom seen anything like that in England. Quite apart from the courtesy, it also tells people who is due to appear that day, and is, of course, an absolute blessing to autograph hunters. Out came their little books when they discovered a name they wanted to add to their collection and an impassioned plea 'just to sign here, please, for my daughter' or whoever. What also struck me about American television studios was the difference in timing schedules, they seemed to be able to alter them without warning. If I am training a dog during a programme in England and my time is up I am faded or signalled out, but I remember going to Washington once for a half-hour programme and being allowed to overrun the scheduled time by over an hour. In New York, I had great fun appearing on the programme, *Tell the Truth,* in which three English women – of whom I was one, of course –, a Rockefeller Institute official, and a secretary were presented to the panel to decide 'which one was the dog trainer'. The night before, these other two women had come to my hotel and I had given them as much instruction as I could on dog training, together with a copy each of my book *Dog Training My Way* to read up overnight. Each member of the panel was allowed three questions. I was not chosen at all. The Rockefeller Institute official was chosen and she must have done her homework thoroughly for she acted out her role very well and they could not stump her on dog training methods. I, at least, won one hundred and fifty dollars and a dress. The dress did not fit me but the money was welcome as we had had to pay for Michael to come with me. All the interviews were fun and the inteviewers well-briefed which made our chats much more interesting.

What also impressed me was the speedy travel by plane. On one of the planes I was on, my nail scissors had at first been taken from my bag and given to the pilot as a safety precaution when I went through the safety check, but then the air hostess, who had recognized me as she had watched one of my programmes on television, told the pilot who I was and my scissors were returned to me. We flew in as many as three planes in a day, starting perhaps in New York and ending up in Texas.

Once, I was doing a phone-in in Atlanta when there was a tornado. The producer told me he did not think that, in the circumstances, there would be many calls that evening. Every few moments, there were warnings of live cables having fallen down and so on, but the questions kept pouring in regardless of the havoc outside. At the end of the programme I was told that I had been asked more questions than any other person. It all goes to show that dog lovers in the States do not mind about tornados as long as they can get an answer to problems about their pets!

One rather interesting thing took place when I was due to appear on the Dinah Shore programme. Her minions had come out of the studio to see whether I was a suitable candidate and I was warned that Dinah Shore had a Basset which was absolutely untrainable. This was a wonderful challenge to me, so I gladly went on the programme and the dog simply did everything that I wanted it to do. It was so quick that I said to Dinah Shore 'Now come along, you learn what to do with your Basset.' The Basset did everything she wanted after that and she was surprised to find that in so few minutes her problem dog had shown that it really quite liked obeying after all – although I believe a disobedient and untrainable dog was part of the set-up of the show.

I had many adventures in the States while I was there. One happened while I was staying in Fort Worth. The news television rang me up to say they would like to take some film to put on their news at lunchtime. Could I find a dog? Well, of course I could not find a dog without going out and looking for one on the streets as I was only staying in a hotel and had never been in the town before. Anyway, I suggested to them that I get in their film van and we toured Fort Worth until I saw somebody with a dog which I thought might be suitable. The young girl I had found had a Samoyed puppy which looked to be about six or seven months old and we stopped the van. I got out, went up to the girl and asked for her help. 'I am Barbara Woodhouse,' I told her, 'and your local television station want to put out a short programme to show how I can train a dog in six minutes.' I had a film unit with me and wondered whether she would let me have her dog to demonstrate with, if it had not already had any training which she assured me it had not. She laughingly agreed and we found a small patch of grass where I gave the dog its training for the camera. I always carried a choke chain and lead in my bag

Impromptu training of the Samoyed puppy at Fort Worth

which made this possible. The dog did everything it was told so, not only were the news cameramen pleased, but the girl also was delighted and when I thanked her for lending me her dog, she threw her arms around my neck and gave me a very warm kiss. Aren't Americans nice?

After that, a lady who had been watching from a window opposite dashed out and asked if I would also train her very naughty Dachshund, so I trained her dog as well. The cameramen filmed this as a bonus and then everyone went home.

Another time we went to stay with a Mrs Watson of Chatanooga. She had met me at Cruft's Dog Show years ago and had asked me to go down and spend the weekend with her if ever I was in her area of the States. While I was there, I witnessed the most amazing sight: a little Yorkshire Terrier was climbing a wire fence just like a monkey. It just stuck its front feet through the holes in the wire and shinned up. I had never seen anything like it before.

We went all over the States and were most warmly welcomed. Americans whom I had met in England or who had seen me on television rang me up and asked us out to lunch.

We went out to lunch with some people who had bought *Talking to Animals* when they were over here. They took us to a Chinese restaurant and there for the first time, I saw plastic bags being handed round to take home the surplus food, even the soup, from our enormous plates. I thought this a sensible idea, but could not see myself going into a restaurant in London and asking for a plastic bag in which to put my soup so that I could warm it up at home for next day's lunch! But that is what people do as a matter of course in the States. The amount of food we were given was one thing that did bother us however. When we asked for a steak we were given meat literally about an inch thick and seven inches across. We felt most embarrassed at first at leaving so much food on our plate. I am not a very big eater; I eat between meals very often but I am not accustomed to eating great quantities. In the end, we found a solution when we ate alone, although it was not always easy when we were in company: my husband would order the meat, I the vegetables and we would then put half of each portion on our plates - though we found it difficult to get vegetables then, as tossed salad was more popular and would be served with every meal without even being ordered. Once,

Mrs Watson of Chattanooga watching her little Yorkshire Terrier climbing the fence - a most unusual sight!

in San Francisco, we ordered one banana split between the two of us. My husband started one end and I the other. Americans certainly seem to have much larger appetites than we do. We found the price of food terribly high. A boiled egg cost about forty-five pence and tea and toast cost eighty pence while dinner cost sixteen pounds for both of us. This may not sound so bad these days but seemed enormously expensive to us in 1973 especially as we had to foot the bill for Michael since Stein and Day were only paying for me.

We even had to pay the shoe-shine boy about forty pence as we had been told not to leave our shoes to be cleaned outside the hotel bedroom door because they would be stolen.

What pleased me enormously in America was the universal greeting 'Have a good day' or 'Have a nice time'. This charmed me always. I wish we could get into the same habit here. One lady rang to say that I had trained her husband's Sheep dog

New-found relatives – Wodehouse and Woodhouse, Frank and Michael

when her husband was over here in the American Army and
would I go and spend the weekend with them. She gave us the
most wonderful time and took us to the local dog training
school for a meal.

During the war I had met an American officer who was
wearing a ring with my husband's crest on it. I discovered his
name was Wodehouse and we corresponded for many years. I
learned that he lived in New Jersey and when his family saw
me on television they again issued me with a warm invitation
to go and stay with them, so we not only met our American
contact of years ago, but the whole of the American side of the
Waterhouse family. His sister had married a Waterhouse, he
was a Wodehouse. They are all distantly related to my
husband as the prefix Water or Wood before house means the
families once had a common ancestor. What was strange was
the general family likeness to my husband; they were all over
six feet with the unmistakable good-looking Woodhouse face.
They told us that the first of the Waterhouse branch went over
to America from England in 1912.

During our tour in America we had always been put up at
very good hotels so, by the time we arrived at our hotel in Los
Angeles, we had already been rather spoilt. The bell boy came
up and said, 'May I have your luggage, Madam' and I sensed
his dismay when I handed him a white plastic bag. We were
taken to a room that was not at all nice. I had a double bed in
the first place, which I do not like as I am always terribly
restless and much prefer single beds, so we went back to the
foyer and told the booking clerk that we wanted a room with
twin beds. This time we were put into a room that had just been
repainted and the smell of paint and the draught were really
wicked. I went back to the clerk the following morning having
had a completely sleepless night and told him that we really
must have a decent room, as we could not stand the ones that
we had been offered. I was so tired by this time that I made it
quite clear we should have to move elsewhere if we ended up in
a similar room to the others. As luck would have it however,
the *Los Angeles Times* that morning produced a whole page

about my work with a photograph. When I went into the breakfast room the chef brought me the newspaper and said 'This is you, isn't it, madam?' I said that it was, and he obviously showed it to the manager because when we went into the new room they had given us, it turned out to be quite magnificent. That was not all. On a table was the most enormous bunch of carnations I had ever seen and a card had been attached, 'With the compliments of the management'. So you see the press does have a pull when you want a nice room.

We spent most of that weekend having a rest by the swimming pool, which was beautiful, and visiting friends near Santa Barbara. One day we came downstairs to wait for our escort, and, while wandering around the hotel shops, we met a lady who had friends in England. We had a lovely chat and she gave us a letter to take home for her. It seemed that wherever we went, we met people we knew. One man came up to me in Denver and said 'You must be Pamela's mother, your voice is the same.' He had met my daughter and her husband in Pakistan! Once, at the Beverley Hills Hotel I got talking to a man while waiting for my husband and found that he came from Denham in Buckinghamshire. Then I went on the *Mike Douglas Show* and found that while I was from Rickmansworth, the conjuring chap alongside me came from Watford!

Most of the dogs supplied for my television demonstrations came from the local lost dogs' homes but I was amazed on one occasion to find that, when I was doing a studio demonstration twenty-five miles away from one I had done on the previous day, the same dogs turned up. When I told the lady who brought them that I was sorry but I only trained untrained dogs and certainly not dogs that I may have trained the morning before, she became very angry. In spite of her protestations, I refused to use the dogs again and we only had about a quarter of an hour before the television programme in which I was due to appear came on the air. The producer of the programme then mentioned that she had a Basset and a St Bernard, both about six months old and wondered whether they would be suitable as they had had no training. An assistant immediately rushed to her home to fetch them. The St Bernard was quite enormous, but charming and readily obeyed my instructions. The only difficulty was that he kept backing towards me and trying to sit on my lap during the final part of the interview!

Another show I went on was with Vincent Price who lived near me at Bushey, and there were three of us from the same area in England. The interview I had with Vincent Price was rather funny. I was, as usual, being interviewed about my work with dogs, and another lady who was supposed to model in ice was also there. They brought in the most enormous block of ice and chisels for her to work with. She was to sculpt a figure in front of the viewers but unfortunately, she was so nervous that she could not answer the questions Vincent Price asked her and the more he tried to help her and put her at ease the more tongue-tied she became. Meanwhile the ice was rapidly melting into water. She tried to do her modelling but the heat of the lamps made the ice melt too quickly and so Vincent turned to me and we chatted about dogs, by which time there was little of the model left.

At the end of our tour we were invited back to the States by the studios on whose shows I had been and this time, Michael was included in the invitation. We were not told, however, that I was not to mention my books and when we went on with the stars of *Alias Smith and Jones,* I mentioned my book. This was a genuine mistake and the girl with us got a ticking-off for not having told me beforehand. I had always hated plugging my own books, never having been allowed to do so, of course, on British television but it is an absolute must when on a promotion tour in the United States paid for by a publisher.

In San Francisco, I did three television shows, three radio talks and phone-ins and eight newspaper interviews in one day. In the evening one of the reporters invited us out to her home for dinner with some of her friends and the following

OVERLEAF *I was whisked from one recording studio to another*

On the 'Tell the Truth' programme in New York

With Diane Marino's Basset and St Bernard brought in at the last moment

With Ben Murphy of 'Alias Smith and Jones' in Chicago

On WBBM with Bob Sanders in Chicago

Sheri Safran and Shelley Goodman, Stein and Day's publicity girls

day, she took us to a dog show where my name was put over the tannoy and two Americans, whose dogs I had trained in England, came up and chatted with us. People would just come and say, 'Pardon me, aren't you Barbara Woodhouse, the dog trainer?' and we would have a lovely chat.

American television is very different in many ways from British television. I never had a rehearsal for anything, all the time I was there. I never knew with whom I was going to be thrown into the deep end. It might be three vets having a discussion or it could be the *Cromies Circle* talking about wild animals or Dr Joyce Brother's programme in New York. The make-up girl offered to make me up which I politely refused as I always do the necessary myself but I did ask for my hair to be combed. This was not possible as the unions did not allow the make-up girl to do hair, so I ended up doing everything myself. Actually, I had a dreadful time trying to keep my hair present-able for all the shows. I never went to a hairdresser as I did not have time and had therefore to sleep with clips in my hair which dug into me at night, if I was to make it look anything like tidy the following day.

Sheri and Shelley, the publicity girls who accompanied us on our tour were tremendously efficient, although sometimes I got nervous for they seemed to leave our departure for the studios to the very last minute, but it all worked out all right. I am the sort of person who gets to the station half an hour before the train is due to leave. We were always on time, however, and I thought the organization of the tours quite marvellous. We became very fond of the girls and hated leaving the United States.

One evening in New York, we met up with some acquaintances who showed us around the city. It was quite wonderful; the only things that were rather nerve-racking were the police and fire engine sirens and the yellow cabs which were most difficult to get into without hurting one's spine.

I had fun one day in Cleveland. A big store allowed me to demonstrate my training method to dog owners on the wide concrete way outside their shops and over fifty people brought their dogs. The United States is a country full of dogs. I believe there are more than fifteen million; even the bell boy at a hotel in Philadelphia came up to me and said he understood I had owned a Great Dane – would I like to go out that evening and see his; he had more than twenty. Unfortunately we could not go as we had too many engagements. In Dallas, however, I did go to a dog training school where three classes were simultaneously in progress and watched their methods. Afterwards I asked the head trainer if there were any untrained dogs there waiting to join a class. He told me there were five so I asked if I could demonstrate my method on them to which he agreed. The people seemed very interested in the speed with which the dogs obeyed.

Only two things marred the promotion tour; the lack of books in the shops where I was supposed to do signing sessions – at least two shops had no books when I arrived as they had sold out – and the theft twice of my money. Once, I had given Michael my handbag while I did a television show and he had put it on the floor beside him. When we returned to our hotel, I found my bag had been robbed of every dollar we had and we were unable to pay for the taxi. So I went to a bookshop and introduced myself to them. They lent me seventy dollars which Stein and Day reimbursed, otherwise I would have been stuck. These thefts occurred because, for part of the tour, we had to make our own way to the appointments. Normally the publicity girl, who usually accompanied us, would have had all the money and this would then never have happened. The second time I was caught was on the way to Chattanooga. I went to pay the hotel bill and put sixty-seven dollars on the desk. I bent down to shut my handbag and the girl asked me for sixty-seven dollars again. I told her that she had already had it, and I did not have any more money. In those few seconds when I bent down to shut my bag, she had obviously pocketed the money. Again I had to borrow money, this time from a friend. I have learned my lesson now.

My only contact with America since these trips was during one of our cruises on the *Canberra*. The ship had run out of water at St Thomas as another liner had bribed the water supply people to give our water to it and we had to go on to Miami to pick up fresh water. I managed, however, to make use of my time by phoning somebody I knew in New York who had wanted to do a commercial with me. He flew down to Miami; we met off the ship and I spent all day doing the commercial with him while the ship took on water and the tourists were being taken round on a sightseeing tour. This saved a special trip out and suited everyone all round. I finished work in the Miami studio at 10 p.m. and had just enough time to get back to our boat, which was due to sail at 11 p.m.

A day in my life

I think very few people of my age would survive the amount I have to do in a day. I sleep very badly as my mind will not stop working, so a lot of my planning takes place at night. I am always longing to get up at about 4 a.m. but have to keep quiet for the sake of the other members of the household. I think few people realize how glorious the scents and quiet of the country-side are at this time of the morning, but then you see, I have been used for twenty years to milking my cows at 5 a.m., then taking my dog and pony out for about six miles before break-fast. When I was filming at the studios which, in the past, took up a large proportion of my working week, the dog was often on call at about 8 a.m. By then, she had had her exercise and was ready to do a hard day's work. I felt fit as a fiddle with all the fresh air I had had, whatever the weather, and the only boring thing was sitting doing nothing, perhaps all that day, in the studios. I found the repetitive rehearsals for the actors or actresses extremely dull and often felt I could have taught a dozen dogs by the time they had got their lines or actions right. I think the life of a human actor or actress must be quite dreadful. Even for a dog, the rehearsals and re-takes kill the spontaneity that goes with 'Take 1'. When I am filming as happened in the BBC series, *Training Dogs The Woodhouse Way,* it is always the first take that is the best with no rehearsals. Had I rehearsed them, the dogs would have been too good too soon and the idea of teaching the training would have been lost. In my second BBC special it was the same; everything had to be 'Take 1' because you cannot breathe up an animal's nose twice as it is a greeting between them and other animals or humans. I must be terrible to work with as I get so impatient with all the fiddling that seems necessary to set up the camera, just as the animal is waiting to do what I want. I am lucky in having been with George Morse, the lighting cameraman, on both the BBC series and the BBC special with animals. He soon learned how vital speed and mobility were in an animal series and never got offended at my urgent pleas to 'be quick, George'. I think people realize how keen I am to get the absolute best out of not only animals but humans and soon pick up the atmosphere of urgency needed in this work.

Since January 1980, when my series first came out, I have been inundated by the press for interviews, which I am delighted to give, but I hate being photographed. Instead of just, say, taking two photographs and going away photographers seem to want as many pictures of me as they take of model girls, and slowly my smile wilts or my face grows stiff, not having been trained in the art of mastering the plastic face which can keep its expression for minutes on end. I suppose few people as old as I am like their wrinkles put onto paper. When I was young, except for a few snapshots on special occasions, I ran away from all photographers. The only photograph I really posed for was one which I sent to a casting agency when I felt I would like to be a cowgirl, in Western films, riding glorious horses out on the range. I got no replies so obviously I was not good enough, and now I am glad, with all my experience of making films, that I was not offered work.

One of the things that keeps me busy is my work as a publisher. My husband puts all the prices on the books which means unwrapping them all, sticking labels on them and putting them back in the packets. I do all the invoices and the book work, and wrap them for posting. I think I could get a job

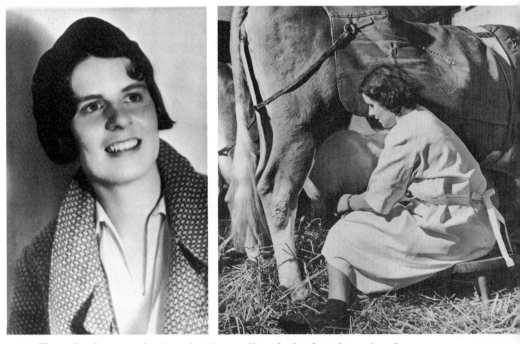

LEFT *The only photograph of me that I actually asked to be taken when I applied to act in cowboy films*
RIGHT *I had always been used to getting up very early to milk my cows*

in a dispatch department if I get too old to do anything else! We all work in our family. Just because I run my businesses from home does not mean I work any less than any commuting family who leave home at 8.30 a.m. and return at 6.30 p.m. As well as my business side, I still have most of the household shopping to do. If I am filming or otherwise occupied, I plan meals a week ahead. I can cook and make things that store well, days ahead whenever I have a minute to spare, I make cakes and stock pile them for the vast number of visitors who come here. I make my own tea time bread too, and I find home-made meringues can soften the hearts of many business men quicker than drinks! I think originally living in the Argentine with the only good shops over one hundred miles away taught me the secret of planning ahead, and of course nowadays, life is made very easy by frozen and tinned foods. The thing is just to add

93

your own ideas to these commodities to make them less conventional. We eat our meals in record time and have an awful job playing with our food if visitors come to a meal, they are so slow. It always seems dreadful that a meal which takes two hours to prepare can be eaten in under fifteen minutes and nothing is left to remember it by except a heap of washing up. Actually, I like washing up. I would not designate this chore to a machine for anything, it is almost a game to see how quickly it can be done. Unfortunately, my eyesight is not as good as it was and, often, a plate is returned to me by a keener eye to be rewashed, and this is a sort of insult! So, maybe, as age takes its toll and I get dimmer-sighted, I shall one day sink to having a washing-up machine in self-defence.

My time is constantly interrupted by phone calls, curiously enough mostly at meal times, so with a quick swallow, I try not to think of my food getting colder and colder as I listen sometimes to interminable stories of how good the dog is before the owner comes to the nitty gritty of how bad it is and what should he or she do. They have seldom read my books or they would know the answer. Sometimes a brief time spent with my book, borrowed from the library, has whetted their appetite to have a chat with me. I like people, and I like talking to people but when you have anything up to three hundred letters a day, it is killing. I have often begged people on television not to write to me with their problems, and soon I shall have to find some method of getting help as both my arms have become extremely painful with muscle cramp from too much typing and writing. The queries that come are all so different it is impossible to have stereotyped replies, and many are more concerned with human worries than canine ones. I get letters from as far away as Saudi Arabia, India, New Zealand, and Australia. The stamps go to my grandchildren. I get invitations to go and stay in many parts of the world including Bogota, but I feel in these troubled days, Croxley Green is probably the safest. I have no wish to be kidnapped in Bogota, suffer an earthquake in Algeria or a typhoon in St Lucia where I was not long before the last one. It seems to me that the world's weather is getting angry. Even in England, the rain seems heavier than it used to be, the winds more gale force, and the vagaries of the climate more violent than in the past, but perhaps I am wrong.

I still find, however, that the weather goes according to plan as of old. For fifteen years now, the days have been fine between 6 and 12 October so when this last BBC film was to be made, I suggested to the producer, Charles Castle, that we film between those dates. The weather, although it poured one night, was fine for the whole six days we were filming, and this makes a tremendous difference to the enjoyment of the superb colouring of the countryside in autumn. One day it was windy and I always take care with animals as when there is a high wind, they hate it and get as irritable as I do; the saying goes, 'never break in a horse in a high wind'. In the last film I had to, but all went well.

I often get asked to do demonstrations of dog training and have done literally hundreds in the past. People often say that obedience trained dogs are not good show dogs. The Bulldog, Noways Chuckles, disproved this. She was Supreme Champion at Cruft's in 1963 and joined my obedience class, becoming a member of my demonstration team on a television show.

Crowds can be a bad influence on dogs. I have often noticed, during my demonstrations, that crowds sometimes prefer a naughty dog to a good one. At one Acton Carnival, my team had just finished a perfect demonstration where every dog did what was required of it except for an Airedale, Jumbo, who belonged to a very nice elderly gentleman called Mr Crew. This Airedale, though he did everything, would only do so in his own time. He came very slowly when called – plod, plod and eventually sat and then went round his owner to heel. Curiously enough, that was the dog that got a tumultuous clap from the audience. The rest of our dogs who had behaved perfectly got a nice polite clap, but nothing like the laughter and applause for the naughty one!

Lots of people come to my home ostensibly to buy the right thick-linked choke chain which shops still refuse to stock in spite of my telling everyone they are the kind ones. When people have bought their choke chain I cannot resist showing the owners how to use it and before they leave, in the few minutes I have had the dog in my home, it has probably had most of the basic training it would need, although the owners need more. This is why I suggest they buy my record *Training Dogs Her Way,* as it would bring my instructions and voice into their own home which, in my opinion, is where a dog should be trained from eight weeks old. I can never see why they wait until six months to take it to a class.

People often write to me for advice and as an added plea, say they are senior citizens. When I reply, I often tell them I can give them at least five years. They must be rather surprised.

I have numerous public engagements and can never find suitable clothes, the colours are drab, the styles are often hideous. As a youngster, I used to design clothes, not only for myself but later for my daughters' special occasions. I am rather careful that what I buy does not put me in the senile category. Once I went to buy an evening dress, said I would

Juno joins me on a brains trust at Norwich

take it, and having asked for a pair of large scissors, proceeded to cut it up to the horror of the saleslady. I then pinned it up showing her how much better it looked worn back to front which was how I always wore it. I often change the unflattering collar line of garments, as my wrinkles appear more and more and I cannot wear open necks. So many dresses have 'V' necks which are particularly unkind to what I call the 'old chicken necks' older people, as well as myself, seem to get. A higher neck line hides the wrinkles.

I have always designed clothes. I designed my own wedding dress as well as my own clothes. During my trip to the Argentine, I met a buyer from a big store in Buenos Aires on board ship. He so admired my clothes that he asked me to design for his shop, but I stuck to breaking in horses.

For my wedding dress, I chose pale blue broderie Anglaise with deeper blue velvet ribbon threaded through the bottom of the skirt. I made a little cap to match the velvet bow at the back. When Pamela got married, I designed Judith's bridesmaid dress which was pale blue and pink with a bustle. I

The bridesmaid dress I designed for Judith when Pamela got married

had a favourite dressmaker at Webbers in Oxford who worked with me and made clothes to my own design. She even made my divided skirts which I always wore when riding in the Argentine.

I have recently had a new design of divided skirt made by a friend, Mrs Elsie Jones in our village, for the BBC film in which I broke in a pony. I did not design this; she very cleverly made it for me. I have a queer idea that horses are easier to break in quickly in a friendly fashion, if you wear ordinary clothes rather than the business-like boots and riding breeches which an unbroken horse is not familiar with. After all, breaking in a pony or horse should be a casual, trusting and friendly affair so I feel informal clothes are best. In the Argentine, a divided skirt was cool to wear, and as a pony was always tied up to our patio for me to ride at any time, a divided skirt (called culottes these days) seemed the ideal thing to wear. It also accustomed the pony to having something flapping all over it, which is excellent.

It is amazing how often I am suddenly rung up to give an interview and have a photograph taken for a newspaper or am asked with only a few hours' notice to go on a television programme or an unexpected person wants to call and my hair looks as if I have been through a barbed wire fence. To have one's hair looking smart is really one of the trials of being on television. I have always got to look right and never have time to do it. One morning a London newspaper, the *Sun,* rang me up and said they wanted to take a photograph of me, and could they come down within the hour? I had not washed my hair for about three days and I looked absolutely ghastly so I went upstairs, washed it, sat outside in the sun with an extension lead on the electricity plug and dried it in half an hour. By the time the press photographer arrived, I was ready with the pins out and prepared for the photograph. It is a bit difficult to be expected to be looking your best all the time; that is the price of so-called fame. Up until recently, I even cut my hair myself. My husband did the back, and I also cut his hair. Most hairdressers either cut too much off and make my husband look like a convict or leave too much on, so I did it to both our satisfaction. Actually, I had a lot of practice in the twenties when I used to cut my sister, Hazel's, hair in a shingle with the horse clippers. I became quite an expert. I like doing hair! Luckily, I was recently asked to a meeting of hairdressers to give a talk on animals. As it turned out, the man who asked me used to be the hairdresser on the P & O liner *Uganda* and he was the only man who had ever cut my hair exactly as I wanted it. I found out that he had retired from the sea to start a little shop at Headington with his wife, so now I go forty miles each way for a hair cut!

My husband and I

We have been married for over forty years and have been exceptionally lucky. Except for one short stay in hospital, we have rarely been separated since the day we were married. Our likes and dislikes are the same and we laugh at the same things. In fact, I really think my husband is rather long-suffering. I make a lot of jokes during the day, some of them may not be funny at all, but he always laughs! We do not go to the theatre, we do not drink and we do not smoke. In fact, people must think our life style extraordinarily dull. But, of course, we do not think that – we are perfectly happy in each other's company. When we married, people said that we looked alike, we might have been brother and sister. Well, we are alike in ourselves now and had no need to celebrate our ruby wedding in August 1980 as every day has been a celebration.

My husband loves animals and we do everything together. He has not got the gift I have, but I doubt if it would be good if we both had it. The three children, Pamela, Judith and Patrick have also not got my gift with animals although they have been good with them most of their lives. When they were young, they spent a lot of time with cows, dogs and horses.

OPPOSITE *Michael and I outside our present Campions*

My son, Patrick, when little, would go down to the field and ride my cows up to the yard without the slightest fear, and the bull used to watch the children having a dip in hot weather in the water tank in the yard. He was very gentle, until one day, a boy put his dog over our fence and it attacked the bull. I had to go in and rescue the boy who had stupidly climbed over the fence to get his dog. From that day on, my bull was not safe with people and had to be sold. When I returned the boy and his dog to his mother, instead of thanking me, she remarked that I looked more like a bull than the bull! I give up!

Judith had her own little dog, Chica, a miniature black and tan Terrier which she trained to go in for top obedience competition work. We used to go round to obedience shows with our two dogs; my Great Dane, Juno, and her tiny Chica. She often beat the Alsatians in Test A. When she first started, Chica was only six months old and Judith six years old. The main problem then was people clapping. The sight of both of them working together brought thunderous applause and once, when Chica had just done a retrieve, the onlookers clapped so suddenly that the little dog got a fright and dropped the dumbbell, which I always thought was very bad luck for Judith. A watching crowd should learn to keep absolutely quiet until the end of an obedience test or the dog may well drop the dumbbell or do something silly. Judith also used to ride her pony with me in the early mornings when I would often ride one of my cows, but she was not as keen on horses as I was.

My eldest girl, Pamela, was always mad on horses and, in this respect of course, she followed in my footsteps. She went to a finishing school in Switzerland, at Chateau-d'Oex, where the headmistress also loved horses. When Madame arrived in London for interviews with parents of prospective students she greeted us, holding in one hand a handbag with stirrup handles. She had a stirrup leather round her suit and we talked, not about Pamela's education but how the children rode and the number of horses they had at the school. When I told her that Pamela had a favourite pony she said, 'Well, why not send it out with Pamela to school?' I thought that would

Judith

Pamela

Patrick

Teaching Pamela to ride Windfall

With Pamela and Judith

Judith aged nine with her six-months-old puppy, Chica, in a demonstration

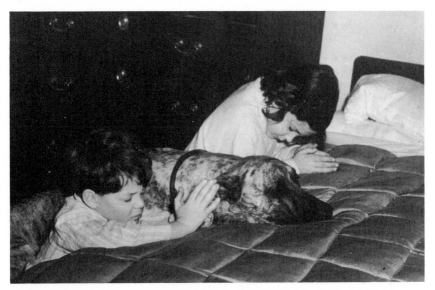

Judith, Patrick and Juno saying their prayers

With Judith and Patrick

Relaxing with Michael, Judith and Chica in the garden at Campions

be lovely so I sent her pony, Freddie, out with her and it nearly broke us financially. The cost of sending the pony out to Switzerland and the forms to fill in, together with the dreadful job of getting it there was very much more than we had bargained for. But I had promised Pamela that it would go with her and we kept our promise. She had a wonderful time at the school with lessons well in second place to riding, although she did, of course, come back speaking fluent French. She rode against the Swiss Army in jumping competitions and beat them. When her two years out there came to an end, we found it impossible to bring her pony home so we reluctantly gave it as a present to the school. I hoped that future pupils would enjoy riding him for he really was a lovely pony. Pamela used to spend much of her free time when she was back, riding in competitions, going to pony camps and doing all the things that the young girls today have a chance to do.

I wish my family had my gifts with animals for there is a tremendous opening in training dogs, but there it is. My little granddaughter, Harriet, however, has a lovely way with dogs and, although she is only seven now, I am hoping that when she grows up, she may carry on and help people with their dogs. She trains her own little dog, Pica, who is a Miniature Pinscher and gives all the right signals in the right tone of voice, and, of course, the dog obviously enjoys it. Perhaps the gift has skipped a generation. There will not be another 'Walkies with Woodhouse' but there may be a 'Walkies with Harriet Walpole'!

Holidays

With the holiday season rushing on us I wonder how many people's hearts sink into their boots as the prospect of being uprooted from a comfortable home draws near. Mine did for one, when the children still lived at home.

I am getting 'set in my ways' as the saying goes. Worse than that, I am a glutton for work, and I cannot imagine any worse hell than enforced idleness. I know sitting on the beach is supposed to relax one's body and mind, but does it? For some people, Atlantic rollers roaring on to the beach can mean little Tommy being swept out to sea, and a slippery jetty can spell danger in the calm waters of Southend or elsewhere. Unless you are the sort of mother who has allowed her child the freedom of the roads in the belief that only by risking its neck will it learn to avoid being run over, in my opinion it is impossible to relax completely when the children disappear round the headland at the seaside.

If one is a good housewife, the meals at most boarding houses or hotels often irritate one. I personally am one of those sinners who eat between meals and a quick cake means more to me when I actually feel hungry than all the meals in Soho. In hotels one cannot go to the larder and grab a snack, and at this sudden change from a longstanding habit my digestive juices rebel. In vain they wait to be satisfied with a snack, and when no snack is forthcoming they try to form an ulcer to pay one out. On the other hand, the owner of such digestive juices may fall into the trap of buying chocolates or ice cream and then the weight goes up.

Now for another aspect of this delightful space of time: holiday exercise. From the word 'go' the children, and possibly Father, are filled with a big desire to take part in everything energetic that was ever invented for the amusement of mankind. It doesn't matter whether you are staying in the Lakes and have a great desire to climb the highest peak, or whether it is the more simple matter of rowing little Tommy round the boating pool. They are both exercises to which our bodies are not accustomed. We have failed, unlike athletes, to go into training for these new efforts. We go all out and then grumble when our aching muscles make themselves unpleasantly known to us. Probably the sun has tempted us to strip our pale bodies with its encouraging warmth, and in an enthusiastic effort to be as brown as the family at the next table, we have stayed too long under its powerful rays. The result is torture when we have to wear our clothes, or torture when we lie in bed. Why don't the creams and balms save us this torture? Why, because we are unwise, but on holiday wisdom is left behind at home.

If we think on holiday we are going to get the 'home-like comfort' advertised, we are sorely mistaken; at home the comfortable bed we have slept in has moulded its springs to our shape – on holiday the hotel beds have so many shapes in them during a season that they can only do their best by being a multitude of ups and downs, and only too well do I know the morning when one wakes up feeling one has at least two displaced discs. Either that or the beds are too narrow or too short. One never realizes beds are made in so many different widths and lengths until one encounters those used in holiday residences. I feel they must have been slightly imperfect throw-outs, like stockings.

Don't imagine for a second if you go on holiday that you will completely forget your work; in no time at all somebody has discovered from the hotel register who you are. In a few hours people, who imagine a doctor's main delight is listening to symptoms of strange diseases, will have cornered my husband and begun their tales of woe. Somebody will have recognized me, and naughty dogs from the bedrooms upstairs will be hauled down to be cured of eating the eiderdown, and as I cannot resist curing a naughty dog, in no time at all there will be an obedience class for dogs on the beach. Helpless, the family looks to me to accompany them to the folderol; I wonder what on earth they want to see such a show for and, with a sinking heart, hand back the last naughty dog to its owner.

I believe that on holiday, one has to be completely unselfish in every respect, for I cannot imagine that in a fairly large family everyone wants to do the same thing. One has to compromise, as unless everyone has been trained from birth to happily give up doing what he wants to do, there is bound to be friction, but that is all part and parcel of the holiday spirit!

In considering this delightful holiday time one must not forget the journey. Unless one is rich enough to travel by plane in comfort, one is either packed into a most uncomfortable railway carriage, or one travels by car on roads fraught with intense danger from the word 'go'. Every fool that ever owned a driving licence seems to be let loose in a car in the holiday season. Traffic hold-ups and rude drivers who turn round and mouth vile epithets at one when they themselves ought to be banned for life from driving, are always in evidence.

Another holiday problem is, what does the average person do with his pets and garden? Is the person entrusted with these precious possessions going to look after them properly? There must be few animal lovers who really happily leave their animals in any one else's care. Yet if they do not, they are tied to a British or Irish holiday, and the delights of foreign travel are barred. I have never yet found complete peace of mind in leaving anything to anyone else, but that is part of the hazards of taking a holiday.

Holidays when our dogs were alive were very different. When we went to Cornwall, the dogs came too and were

Michael, the children, our dogs and I on our way to Ireland for a holiday

welcome everywhere. As the children got older, my husband would take Judith abroad by himself. I used to stay with the dogs. I would never have put my dogs in kennels as there is no way a dog can tell that you are coming back. I stayed at home for twenty-one years until the last of my four beloved Great Danes died. Most of our holidays since then have been on cruises, although there was one occasion earlier on when I was able to make satisfactory arrangements at home and my husband and I went to Switzerland. We stayed at Interlaken and set off at eight each morning in the train to make different excursions. One day, we travelled up to Kleine Scheidegg but the height was too much for my husband. He felt nauseous and we were preparing to go down when I saw a shop that sold souvenirs. I asked how much some colour postcards were and was quoted an outrageous price. I spoke to my husband in German and the woman in charge quickly changed her tune and said, 'I will let you have it for . . .' quoting a much smaller sum, which all goes to show how tourists are always rooked. It was June and the gentians were wonderful. I picked one carefully with its roots intact and kept it in my sponge bag in the hotel and throughout our journey home. It thrived at Campions for about seven years. I have never been back since, but I would dearly like to. It is a place where I could happily retire. The mountains recharge my batteries, they remind me of the lovely Wicklow Mountains and recapture the joys of those early days for me.

We have spent a number of Christmases on the SS *Canberra,* going on wonderful cruises where we could rest and get sunburnt as the ship headed across the Atlantic for warmer climes. Those were the days when most ships had two classes, first and second. We would always travel first class which was pleasant and not overcrowded. We could watch entertainments comfortably and there was always a seat vacant. Now these ships are one-class. Swarms of people come in to all the entertainments so that one cannot get near and the atmosphere is far from relaxing. At one time, the same people would come every Christmas and we got to know them and would wait for them at Southampton. It was quite like a family party. Now it is all more like Butlins-on-Sea. We tried other ships but the same masses spoilt our peace, until we discovered the educational cruise on the *Uganda.* However improbable it may seem, one thousand school children and three hundred passengers made a delightful fortnight. We went to original places with excursions included in the fare. The children in no way disturbed us as they occupied a different part of the ship and we could go down and listen, if we wished, to their very interesting lectures, or we could stay in our own part of the ship and mix with charming, mostly retired people. The amusements were not professional, simply consisting of films and the usual entertainment on board ships. The crew provided some excellent evening entertainment which I consider might well be seen in some of London's variety shows. There were plenty of games, swimming and diversions as well. Until recently, I felt sure that it was the

Just Barbara

Winner of the first prize as the 'common cold' in the fancy dress contest on the P & O Oriana

best holiday for tired people who wanted to get away for a while (as I do) from the endless telephone, and letters. Unfortunately, this cruise is also becoming too popular. I do not know what we shall do in the future, especially as we seem to have been to all the places that these ships visit.

One year I was bitten by a schizophrenic Bulldog who had been perfectly good all day and was let loose with all the other dogs in the field. He suddenly got up behind me, got hold of me and bit my arm to the bone. When I managed at last to prise him away, he got hold of my finger and bit that to the bone too, so I was completely crippled. Luckily, I escaped being permanently injured. Had the teeth gone a few millimetres more, my tendons would have been severed and I might not have had the use of my right arm and hand again. At that moment, the injury meant that I could not do any of my work, so I suddenly decided to go on the P & O *Oriana* for a cruise, and take my son, Patrick, with me as he was on holiday and could help me since I could not dress or bath myself or anything. My husband was too busy working at the hospital. So we set off and it was one of the nicest cruises I have been on in all my life. Somehow, all the people seemed to be laughing and jolly and happy and Patrick looked after me so marvellously. Had I had a trained nurse, I could not have been better looked after. He bathed me, dressed me and was always hopping back to see that I was happy and contented (which I was, as there were some very pleasant people on board). He had quite a good time as well because there were also a large number of young people around. Towards the end of the cruise, an amusing fancy dress competition was held on the ship and I went as the 'common cold'. I wore a dressing gown, painted my nose with lipstick, draped paper handkerchiefs round myself and hot water bottles and medicines plus anything else I could rake up from the doctor on the ship. I won first prize in my class and Patrick won first prize in his. I took the metal iron holder off the ironing board for him, put it round his face, got him some scruffy clothes and a label which read, 'Behind the Iron Curtain'. We had great fun and I shall remember the cruise to my dying day, in spite of my injuries which healed up in about six weeks.

If I am ever free from phone calls, I hope to do a lot more travelling abroad. I want to go to South Africa and Australia and spread my training methods there and perhaps go back again to America, but at present I live for today, tomorrow never comes.

Television and unexpected success

What saddens me personally is the unbelievable jealousy that some people have shown in writing to newspapers or to me about the gift that I have for training dogs. A few trainers have said the most dreadful things about my television series. Things like, 'She's no good: don't follow her advice.' 'You could easily choke your dog by putting the choke chains on upside-down.' (I do not deny that, which is why I always demonstrate the correct way of puting them on.) 'Don't pay any attention to how Mrs Woodhouse teaches you to train your dog with a choke chain' . . . In my series, I most painstakingly explained that a choke chain must never be left on a dog or used as a collar. If put on correctly and never closed on the neck, it in no way hurts any dog as long as you have the right thick-linked choke chain. I have often demonstrated this by jerking the choke chain on my own bare arm to show it does not produce a mark of any sort. I cannot understand how these people can bother to write to newspapers and how newspapers can even print these things when they are practically libellous.

OPPOSITE *With Bernie Winters and Schnorbitz after having been presented with the Female Television Personality of the Year award 1980 by the Writers Guild of Great Britain and Pye*

I was consulted recently by a few newspapers about a Border Collie which had savagely attacked a child who, as a result, had needed one hundred stitches in its head. They wanted my opinion about Collies. I told reporters who rang me up that some Working Collies had a nervous temperament and could be dangerous with children. We, ourselves, had been brought up with Sandy, a big rough Collie, who did not like strangers and I have met a number of people in my training years with nervous Working Collies inclined to bite. What I did tell the newspapers, not a single word of which was printed, was that 'some' Working Collies were like this. The newspapers simply mentioned 'Collies' and there are several breeds of these. People took it that I meant all Collies and wrote me some of the rudest letters imaginable, claiming that I had caused Collies to be put down and goodness knows what. I do not believe that Border Collies make good household domestic pets. Their lives should be spent on farms, where they cover perhaps twenty to thirty miles a day, working sheep with the full co-operation of their master. I do not believe that they are happy being played with and mauled by children and having no work to do. They are very intelligent dogs and tremendously easy to train, which is why I did not include one in my television series. They are too easy. It always worries me that most of the trainers in this country today who compete in obedience tests use Border Collies. Why don't they use dogs that are a little more difficult to train so as to show off their skill?

I have a stand at Cruft's Dog Show every year where I have a tremendous signing session of all my books and I also take along my choke chains and leads. It is a good opportunity to meet dog lovers from all over the place. For two days, I very often start at eight in morning and do not finish until nine in the evening. Though I enjoy it enormously, I find it tiring as it is naturally a very noisy place with people firing questions at me as I am trying to sign about twelve books at once.

My commitments are widely varied. In the freezing cold last November, I sat with a lot of dogs in a float being driven

Helping Sureweld raise £1,000 for the Jimmy Savile appeal for Stoke Mandeville Hospital

around a town, advertising a fair in aid of Jimmy Savile's appeal for Stoke Mandeville Hospital. I am often being asked to do comic television shows where I appear to be more of a comedian than a dog trainer. I do not know what the public reaction to this is but I enjoy it. I am asked to open dozens of fêtes, present prizes to schools and help charities galore, all of which naturally I cannot do. I do not think people realize that I am over seventy-one! I am always being asked to go on dog walks for charity but, once again, I feel I am a bit past it!

Letters from viewers tell me of the reaction of their dogs to my shows:

'You might be amused at what has just happened. My two cross-breds who were having their meal in the kitchen, a most important moment in the day, heard your voice, left their food and came into the living room to put their noses against the screen!'

LEFT *Dr Johnson's Hoopy watching himself being trained on my television series*
RIGHT *Terry Wogan and I being closely watched on television by the Pekinese, Saku and Tai*

I have lots of photographs of dogs watching the television series I did. One photograph of two little Pekinese, shows how the dogs concentrated on the Yorkshire Television programme, *Don't Just Sit There.* We tried an experiment; I was ten miles away with outside broadcast cameras and the dog I was to have was in the studio. I gave commands to the dog from ten miles away. The dog heard, saw me on the screen in the studio and after peering round the television set to see where I was, obeyed all my commands instantly.

Another instance which stays clearly in my mind dates back to much earlier years. I remember I was at Oxford by the river and, on the other side of the bank stood a man with his Alsatian. Well, I have always been very fond of Alsatians, or German Shepherds as they are now termed, and called out, 'Hello boy' in a nice bright voice. He immediately plunged into the river and came over to me. The man was absolutely furious and called him back. I apologised to him and told him that I could not resist talking to an Alsatian. He replied that he had never seen his dog go to anyone else in his life and I explained that I thought it was my tone of voice and suggested that I called it back again. He assured me that this would not happen a second time, I bet him five pounds that it would! The man agreed and so I called the dog back again. It instantly plunged straight into the river and came to me. Unfortunately, the man was on the other side so I could not collect my five pounds!

I think the most unexpected thing that has happened to me was receiving a letter asking me to attend the luncheon of the Screenwriters Guild and the Pye Television Award. I refused the invitation saying that I was too busy to come. About a fortnight later they rang me again to ask if I was sure that I could not attend as they wanted me to give a prize to somebody. I thought it rather churlish of me to refuse as I did not actually have an engagement on that day and so agreed to go, never guessing, of course, what the result of this would be. When I reached Marylebone station with my husband, I was met by one of the organizers of the luncheon and in the car going to the Hilton Hotel, he told me that it was I who had been chosen to receive the Female Televison Personality of the Year award. Well, you could have knocked me down with a fly-paper! Never in my life did I think that a dog trainer would receive this tremendously complimentary award. I was so grateful I could hardly speak. Anyway, I accepted it at the lunch with great joy on behalf of all the dog owners who have been kind enough to go through my hands and all the people who have listened to me on the radio and television about training their dogs in the hope that my motto, 'Dogs should be a joy to all and a nuisance to no one' would eventually come true.

This award, of course, meant that I was overwhelmed with photographers. I was taken to Hyde Park and photographed with that delightful personality, Bernie Winters and his dog, Schnorbitz, from every possible angle. I realize now what model girls have to endure to get the right angles for the photographs. 'Look here, Mrs Woodhouse, no here, *here,* over here, Mrs Woodhouse'. Although I loved the publicity, by the time they had finished with me I did not know whether my face was looking upwards, downwards or sideways!

Of course, there is no doubt that all the sudden publicity arose from my series on BBC television. This did not however happen by itself with an 'out of the blue' invitation. Mother's description of me as a young girl had always been 'Barbara will fall over every fence and pick herself up'. No truer description was ever given to anyone. All my life I have fallen down or been knocked down by people, metaphorically speaking, and had the task of setting myself up again. No particular type of person or thing has done this to me, but it seems my lot is to be a hard one, nothing has ever been put on my plate without my working terribly hard for it. That is why, when some people say, 'How lucky you are to have such a wonderful home, husband, etc.' I disagree with them. Luck does not come into it; most of it was gained by just really hard work. It was I who had for more than ten years perpetually written to the BBC suggesting a series. I then wrote personally to Bill Cotton telling him that I had very much enjoyed *One Man and His Dog* and their sheep herding, but that I spent my life training dogs not to chase sheep and felt viewers would be interested in a dog training series. It worked and a producer called Peter Riding came to see me, but the series took nearly a year to set up. We asked for volunteers to be trained with their dogs and were inundated with replies, more than 2,700 in all. All sorts of different dogs, Afghans, Salukis, Beagles . . . were selected to be filmed so that the dog-owning public would realize that it is possible to train every breed of dog. It all turned out to be an enormous success which is what I hoped, but it far exceeded my wildest expectations. To be recognized and known wherever I go and to have received an accolade like the Female Television Personality of the Year award was something I never dreamed would happen to me. It is fun. I love people, and

OPPOSITE *The Duke of Bedford slipping Juno a bone at a charity luncheon*

having lots of bits of paper thrust in front of me to autograph. I love waving to lorry drivers who yell 'walkies' from their cabs, shaking hands with complete strangers and even waving to passengers in a slow train passing through a station. All this has happened to me and much more. The words 'sit!' and 'walkies' have become so popular it really is funny. A little girl walked into our drive the other day, picked up some gravel and said to her small friend, 'Look, I have got Barbara Woodhouse gravel' which made me laugh.

Recently radio and television have kept me busy so when Roy Plumley asked me if I would choose my favourite records for his *Desert Island Discs* programme, I had great fun going through all the tunes I had enjoyed throughout my long life. It really made me feel quite weepy to hear the finished programme, remembering all those beautiful days that have gone by when music really was music. Some listeners of my generation shared my choice, they said, with great pleasure. 'In a Monastery Garden' seemed a favourite tune of the olden days when I was young.

I now get asked to do commercials for most unlikely things (all turned down). I get begging letters, nice letters, rude letters. I get some lovely press write-ups and some rude and untrue ones. I meet ninety-nine and a half per cent pleasant people and a half per cent horrid people who try to make me rise to their unfavourable comments. If I go to a dog show only for my own pleasure, dozens of people beg me to help them with their problem dogs and I give help freely, but as I am now allergic to dogs, despite being immunised against this trouble, I usually come out in large bumps at the show. I hope nobody has noticed me scratching! It is all in a day's work and all I hope is that I can go on for years and years doing what I love, being with animals and people.

OPPOSITE ABOVE *At the opening of a fête at Chatsworth with the Duchess of Devonshire*
BELOW *Sporting my T-shirt on a programme with Magnus Pike*

125

My books and charity cards

My first two books were turned down by publishers and I had to take the risk of publishing them myself, while at the same time borrowing money; all of which I found very difficult to do. Eventually, I took all my books over from commercial publishers and started my own concern. I had no idea how many books I would sell. More than anything, I found the tremendous sweat of going round all the shops a strain. I had to locate the book buyers and received tremendous slaps in the face, (metaphorically speaking), from some of them which, at first, discouraged me. They seemed somehow to think I was hawking round unsaleable books. Looking back now I think it was a bigger challenge than I had realized. Eventually they accepted my books and found they actually did sell.

Nowadays, my publishing business is an absolute money-spinner. In the last six months my turnover has been over £40,000. At first, publishers brought out my books but as they went out of print I re-published them myself, taking over from Fabers and Max Parrish ... I have written and published eight books entirely by myself. The last but one, called *Almost Human,* about my Great Danes was rather amusing. I was

OPPOSITE *Publicity photo for my first book*

127

asked by a publisher to do a book for him. He said, 'Do write a book for our firm one day, Barbara.' I told him that I liked publishing my own books but he insisted, so I sat down and wrote *Almost Human* in a few days and sent it to him. I thought it was a pleasant informative and interesting book and that he would like it. It came back rejected about a month later so I rushed off to my own printers, published it and sold 8,900 copies in twenty-one days. Of course I had the most fantastic publicity on *Nationwide,* Hughie Green's show and in the press, so publishers are not always right!

To any of my readers who think they, too, might be interested in publishing their own books, my warning would be to be very careful. You can lose a lot of money in this game. You must choose something that you are pretty sure people will want to hear about because the risks are terrific. Not only have you got to pay out money before you have probably sold a copy but you have also to pay your printers very promptly. You must have somewhere to store your books because the cost of storing these days will quickly take away your profit and that means your turnover has got to be very quick. You must never send your books out on sale or return as returned books will probably come back to you dirty and you would have to throw them away or sell them so cheaply that you would be better off throwing a certain amount of them away. I recommend cash with the order or pro formas. You have to put up quite a lot of money sending out books for review. Some people write and ask you for a copy, but all they really want is to add your book to their shelves. Books sell by word of mouth as much as they do through enthusiastic reviews. Something that needs the closest attention is the printing of your book. The correction of your proofs and the layout need skill and you may have to learn by bitter experience as I have done. Although now I have a very happy arrangement with my present printers, I have in the past been done in the eye due to bad workmanship without any recourse to law. I once had to throw twelve thousand copies of my books into the dustbin because the covers that had been recommended to me had faded. Now I have all my

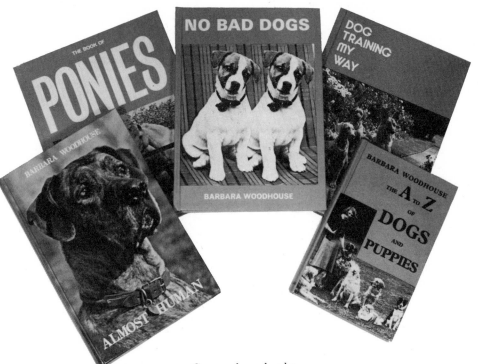

Some of my books

book covers laminated which is what I had originally asked for but had then been dissuaded from. As usual I was right. Use your own ideas, do not be put off by those who only appear to know better and if possible design your own covers. I keep the copyright of all my books, which is most important.

One of the pitfalls of being your own book selling representative is the cost of getting around. Traffic wardens are not always susceptible to a claim that 'one is unloading' when only two books come out of the back of a van! I have a goods licence on my car but was given a parking ticket the other day when I was taking money into our local bank – a matter of minutes only. I appealed but did not get anywhere. On the whole, though, if I may digress for a minute – which I am more inclined to do, I am afraid, as I get older! – I have always found traffic wardens extremely pleasant and understanding. In

130

fact, I must be one of the very few people who has received Christmas cards from traffic wardens all over the country. Once, I had to leave my dogs in my car on a hot day to attend court. I asked the warden if she would give me a little time if I was held up, and also open the windows for my dogs if it got too warm. When I came back, she had opened the windows and there was no ticket. On another occasion, in Leicester, I lost my husband whom I had left in the car while I went off to a bookshop. When I came back I could not remember where I had left him, let alone the car in which he was sitting patiently. I appealed to a warden, saying, 'I can describe the car and my husband. Can you possibly help me?' She was most helpful and found them for me. One traffic warden in Bristol actually got in our car to show us the shop we were looking for as the one-way system there is very difficult to explain.

In publishing my first two books independently I ran up against all the snags involved in marketing one's own product. Buyers looked askance at me when I said I represented myself, but they did, in the end, buy my books. Recently one buyer who did not want my book and said so quite rudely, got a shock when a lady at one end of the shop said 'Hello Mrs Woodhouse, I have got all your books'. I told her she had not as I had just published another and, if she liked to come outside, I would show it to her, which she did. I sold it to her on the doorstep of the shop in full view of the bookseller – very naughty! I love the challenge of selling things and believe that the greatest asset a sales representative can have is a good memory. I have a first class memory, though it is not as good now as it was, and I love talking to book buyers, being careful to remember, not only their individual names but also some of the things they talk to me about. Some time ago, I was in a shop and the buyer had a dreadful cold. I remembered that the last time I had called, she also had a cold so I commented on

OPPOSITE *Collecting for the blind with Patrick in London*

Charity Christmas card of Moor Park sold for Guide Dogs for the Blind

this and we chatted about the horrors of the perpetual cold. The atmosphere was decidedly friendly as we parted. It is so much more fun like this. Selling things is always fun, although book selling can be a very difficult job with book buyers being out at lunch at different times or out to the dentist, having tea breaks, or not being available to see travellers on that day. I am really sorry for some representatives as they always seem to be kept waiting. I was lucky in that I had only one set of titles to show anyone and buyers usually saw me very quickly, especially as I carried the books around with me and delivered them on the spot. That saved expensive postage. I now no longer act as my own representative as orders come through without my doing anything, but I enjoyed it while it lasted.

Selling Christmas cards was another challenge. The sale of charity cards before Christmas is run like a full battle waged in your letter box, at your door and by every other legal means known to the organizers.

I was one of those involved in calling on people door to door, carrying my Guide Dog Christmas cards with me. It can be work with very rewarding results but it can also be work in which one's patience is tried almost beyond endurance.

At least one in six door-bells are out of order, and the knockers are so stiff that if you do manage to get a bang, the result is deafening. The housewife rushes to answer the door, and is somewhat let down to find it is only a request to buy Christmas cards instead of the house burning down.

One has no hope of selling anything if an au pair girl answers the door. Her mistress simply sends the reply, 'Not today, thank you'. If the 'daily' answers, she does not consult her mistress at all, she just says, 'No thank you' and shuts the door in your face. Men are very doubtful backers of the cause.

The most generous supporters are the young housewives, either because they are still young enough to feel charitable or they have not yet learned the lightning art of refusal. If there's a dog in the house, and it receives the collector (me) with open arms and a thunderous welcome as so many of these extraordinary animals do instead of biting one, the owner is lost. It is perfectly obvious the collector has to be supported to get rid of her and her unwelcome attentions to your dog whom you previously thought only loved you.

Children are a tremendous help as they snatch the cards from the collector's hands and cover them with sticky fingers, so the packet is ruined and the mother has to buy it, or they start screaming if they want the cards and, though mother will not give in to them at first, they always win in the end.

Sometimes the collector has to be a jack of all trades to win support for her fund. I have had to mend a gas stove for an American housewife, tune a Mini's carburettor, give five sharp training minutes to a delinquent dog and agree to try and find a wife for a young man of twenty-eight whose mother was a bit tired of cooking for him. At one house I patiently waited while an old gentleman finished a telephone call, upon which he turned to me, grabbed my hands and planted a kiss on my cheek saying, 'That was a call from my son in New Zealand – he's engaged to be married'. Only when he realized that I was a complete stranger, did he apologise for his enthusiasm, but I was so pleased he was so happy I would have probably kissed him if he had not got in first.

The weather makes an awful lot of difference to the sale of Christmas cards. I used to pray for rain. When I arrived on doorsteps dripping from every hair on my head, removing the cellophane wrapping from the packet covered in raindrops, it all helped the psychological aspect of selling. It takes a hard heart to refuse to support a cause carried on under such trying circumstances.

One householder had for two years in succession informed me as she opened the door that her children had measles, hoping I would fly away. I wondered if she would do the same the following year. Some would say they had already bought the card elsewhere, which could not be as I had published this particular card myself.

One very charming lady thanked me for giving her the chance to buy the cards and many said how lovely they were. Another lady, however, whose husband had answered the door refused to buy any cards as there was not a picture of cats on them.

I have even committed the terrible crime of forgetting the number of the last house I called on the previous day, with the result that I have knocked again the next day only to be greeted with a cold rejection. I have been asked into houses and have had the most enjoyable chats, only spoilt by the knowledge that I was losing about fifty pence in sales for every five minutes I gossiped.

I have heard the marital troubles of an absconding husband at number ten only to meet up with the woman he absconded with at number twenty-eight, and listened to both sides of the story in one afternoon! No one can say selling Christmas cards for charity isn't one of the most entertaining and happy ways of helping those unfortunate people who need help. Peace, goodwill towards men and, we hope, the well-meaning collector as well.

Ninety-nine per cent of the people I called on were charming and generous, and I really looked forward to my annual meeting with them. I shall certainly be kind to those who call on me, when charity certainly will begin at home!

The Ps have it

Recently, I gave a talk to a branch of the Institute of Management on selling which I greatly enjoyed. They asked me what I thought were the most important requirements for success in business. Looking back on that lecture I now realize that most of the guidelines I chose begin with the letter 'P'.

To start with, you do not have to be rich. You had much better be *Poor* or fairly *Poverty* stricken. I think you have got to know your own *Potential*, develop your *Personality*, have *Push* and *Persistance*. *Pretend* you are bigger than you are because, if you are always excusing yourself or apologising you will not get anywhere. You have got to have a good *Phone* manner. There is nothing more annoying than listening to a voice that grates. You have got to be able to *Produce* interesting things for the *Press*, including good *Pictures*. You want to know which side of your own face is *Photogenic*, and you have to be terribly *Patient* with *Photographers*. You must persuade them to take you at your best angle. I always manage to get them to take me full face which is best for me. You cannot succeed without the help of the *Press* and *Publicity*. You can work all your life, but the day you need a *Press-cutting*

OVERLEAF *Surrounded by Plenty of Paraphernalia in my office*

135

agency you are on the bottom rung of the success ladder. Do not ever expect *Praise* when you are doing anything, especially in films and television. In the past, my dog did many films, television programmes and commercials but only got praised by the studio technicians who were always ready to clap her. Directors are so full of their own problems that they forget.

Another thing you have got to do is to take the *Plunge*. I made a second feature for the cinema which nearly bankrupted me and almost lost me my house. This plunge meant that I had to borrow from the bank and did not get the film released until some time afterwards. I was overcharged for everything and it was not a very pleasant experience. Another thing you should do, always give very *Prompt* replies and acknowledgment, not only to letters but for little presents. I get presents from people who want to show their gratitude and I always reply at once with great enthusiasm which is the least I can do to show my appreciation. Try to remember the names of *People* you come in contact with. I am afraid I am becoming very bad at this. I am inclined to say 'Hello' and carry on talking and then when I see them again, I cannot remember their names. Always appear *Pleased* to meet whoever is being introduced to you. Look them straight in the face and treat them as though each is the most important person on earth. I am sure it gratifies people. And if you possibly can, laugh with them.

I try to keep my *Prices down*. I think that my hardback books must be some of the cheapest books on the market. Of course, I have published them myself and I am able to decide how much *Profit* I want. In my case it is very low because I do not spend a lot and I do not need a lot. I have had nearly everything I need in life and I would prefer people to be able to afford to take in the knowledge which I have put into my books to help them train their dogs and ponies. You may not be able to stand some of the people you meet, but you have just got to tolerate them. Try to do this with a smile or you are not going to get on very well. Finally, try to come up with a *Product* that is within the *Purchasing Power* of the *Public*. Last, but not least, I shall finally *Prepare for Paradise*.

Love me and don't hate my dog

It is very sad that there are restrictions on where dogs can go these days. In the old days, my animals could go everywhere with me, but now in the interests of hygiene, 'Dogs are not admitted' read the notices in the shops. To my mind, it is much more unhygienic to have people sneezing over your cake or pie or touching them with unwashed hands than having a quietly-behaved animal sitting in a corner.

People have reacted very strongly to dogs now and I think it is understandable. Clive James was right in his claim that you cannot walk on pavements these days because dog owners do not train their dogs properly, but then, of course, you cannot only blame the dogs but also the indifferent owners for their disregard of the public and cleanliness. Perhaps parks should be divided and half declared no dog areas, like smoking and non-smoking train carriages.

In the last few years there has been a hate campaign going on about dogs. This was mainly due to the media and I suppose came to light when a columnist wrote an article on how horrible dogs were. This was followed up by a television programme which caused parents to be anxious about the risks involved in owning a dog to the health and hygiene of family and home. This is totally exaggerated. There is no risk at all if all the necessary precautions are taken to see that a

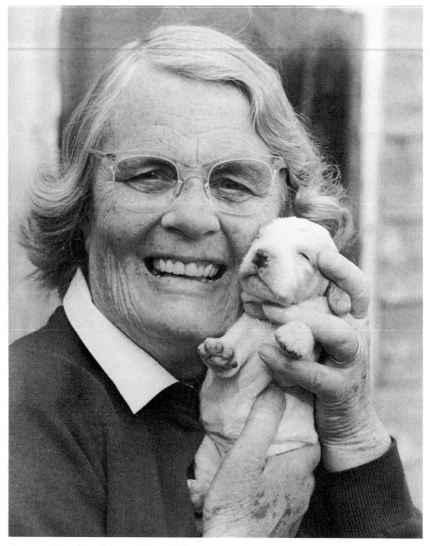

A new friend, only ten days old

dog is worm free. *Toxocara canis* is what the problem is all about but it can only be passed on to a human if he *eats* the eggs of the worms that remain in the faeces in the soil. It could, therefore, be passed to children and could cause blindness in one eye but the chances of this happening are infinitesimal if sensible precautions are taken and children made to wash their hands thoroughly before eating. Many viewers had their dogs put down for no reason after watching the television programme and I was constantly phoned by people and the press about it. However, out of fifty million people, the only cases I have been able to trace in the last three years number eleven. Most of the big London hospitals have never seen a case and my husband who had been on the staff of the Western Ophthalmic Hospital for twenty-six years has also never heard of a case. Furthermore had a case occurred, I am sure his colleagues would have told him as they know his wife works with dogs.

It is not possible, in the laboratory, to tell the difference between *Toxocara catis*, from cats, and *Toxocara canis*, from dogs. Both dogs and cats relieve themselves in the earth and cover it up so children playing in sandpits could easily come across the faeces of a cat in a playground and could be infected by putting their hands near their mouths. I cannot believe that many children would put their faeces-soiled fingers in their mouths.

The safeguard is for all dogs and cats to be wormed once or twice a year and for all strays to be rounded up, then this *Toxocara canis* scare would completely disappear. It does not come under the Notifiable Disease Act so that hospitals cannot give the number of known cases and I have seen letters from four major hospitals in London who have never seen a case.

The scare has been grossly exaggerated by people who probably hate dogs and spread fear among the dog-owning public out of all proportion to the necessity for the safety of their children and anybody else's. It has never been a major risk and sensible ownership is the answer. But I do think that something drastic has to be done about the soiling of streets and public places by dogs.

Animal and other stories

Lots of children write or phone me asking for advice on ponies. I do want to give advice to the growing number of animal-struck children there are around, many of whose parents phone me to ask how they should go about finding work in stables for their girls.

The chance of having a career with animals is very slim these days. Hundreds of horse-crazy girls want to work with horses in riding stables. To all of them I say:

By all means do it, but it is a very over-crowded occupation. From the very beginning when you start earning money, put a little aside so that one day, if humanly possible, you can own an animal of your own. However much you enjoy working with horses, you will never get that insight into a horse's mind working with other people's animals. But remember, owning a pony is a big responsibility, it cannot just be left in a field without constant food or care. It might fall ill and certainly it is not cheap to own a pony, what with stabling, vet's fees and blacksmith costs, so think hard before you buy.

I was most amused to hear a 'dog' story from dear old Mattie, otherwise known as A. E. Matthews, the actor. He had a Kerry Blue and another small dog, which was given to him in London by a lady who had a Rolls-Royce. This small dog had always been used to being fed in the Rolls-Royce with the engine running and, unless the engine was on, it would not eat. So when Mattie adopted this dog, it went on hunger strike until he started up the engine of his own car, put the dog and its food inside and all was well.

Another time, I went to a dog biscuit luncheon for a celebration. The chairman got up and said that these dog biscuits were perfectly fit for human consumption. He picked one up and took a bite. Unfortunately, he had false teeth which stuck in the biscuit and he had to go out, leaving me to carry on with stories and chat while the poor man rescued his teeth from the dog biscuit.

I had a lot of happy experiences when going around the country with my Great Danes. One day, Southern Television booked me into a hotel when I was due to appear on one of their programmes. When I arrived there, I told the manager that my dog would freeze if the central heating was turned off at midnight. By that time, Junia was so well known that the manager was quite prepared to leave the heating on all night 'for a film star'. That night, the shop opposite the hotel was burgled. I heard the crash and Junia nearly went mad sensing that here at last was her chance to catch a criminal, but I had no telephone in the bedroom to call the police and could not find the landing light. I saw the thieves stealing television sets but could not do anything about it.

Fairly recently, a lady wrote to me and said she had the nastiest Corgi in the whole of England. It bit her and everyone who came to her house. As she was seventy, she was making her will and leaving the Corgi to me since she thought I was the only person who would be able to manage it!

I receive a lot of funny letters, such as an order for one of my books from a member of the Seafarer's Association in London asking for my book *Dog Training My Way*. Seadogs?

One lady came to my training school with a very nervous Dachshund. I put a choke chain on it and it lost its nervousness so I told her to take it into the show ring with the choke chain on – regardless of criticism. As she entered the ring a large lady with several Dachshunds exclaimed, 'Good

143

heavens, you can't put a great choke chain like that on a little dog; my goat wears a thinner one than that!' My pupil won first prize and the large lady did not win anything. As my pupil went past the large lady and out of the ring, she remarked to her, 'Bring your goat next time!'

The importance of your tone of voice when speaking to animals (or human beings for that matter) was made very clear to me when I was in Gambia a few years back. I went to the Abuco rain forests where the nature reserves are. In a cage, was a hyena which had continued, ever since its captivity to throw itself from one end of it to another hoping to escape. It did this twelve hours a day. Nothing could persuade it to stop, in its misery and fear. I asked the keeper who was there if he would allow me to go and talk to the hyena. He said I could, so I went over to it and in what I call my 'little voice' (which is a fairly soft high-pitched tone) I said, 'Come along, come along.' It stopped throwing itself against the cage and came up to me. It raised its nose to mine, put its ears flat against its face in what I call the 'soft look' which means that the animal welcomes you, and actually wriggled as it came up to me, laid its head against my chest and breathed up my nose. Then it lay down at my feet. I was so amazed at the reaction of this animal that I asked the keeper if I could go out to the reserve where there were many more hyenas and he said I could. I was not allowed in with them, so I stayed outside the wire, and again used my 'little voice' to call them which, incidentally, my mother always asked me to use in the old days if there was any unhappy dog in the boarding kennels. She would say, 'Go and talk to the dog, Barbara, in your "little voice" – it always makes them happy'. Well, I called the hyenas, and one by one, they all came up to me, laying their heads as near to mine as they could and breathing up my nose. One got near enough to push up the wire and lay its head on my chest, and then the whole lot came up, breathed up my nose and laid down at my feet.

Later on that day I went with an expedition to a big reservoir which was very beautiful. I was standing on some concrete when a praying mantis ran out. I had never seen one

Training the praying mantis

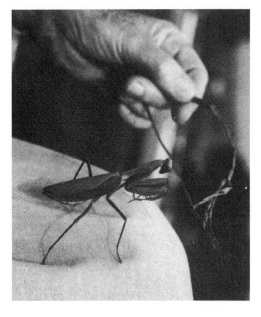

before; it looked like a locust to me but green, rather like an enormous grasshopper. It was terrified of all the tourists and raced about so I said jokingly to them, 'If you all stand still, I will train it for you.'

I managed to get within a few inches of it and told it to, 'Sit and stay' with the 'sit and stay' signal I use for dogs. It looked at me, stopping in its tracks. I then said, 'Lift up your feet. Higher, come on. Sit up', because I knew that praying mantises' sit up on their hind legs. It lifted its feet up and I said, 'No, higher'. We got some perfect photographs of this strange creature obeying my commands with its feet lifted high in the air. Then I was asked to put it on a white coat as it would photograph better, so I picked it up. It had no fear and again, it obeyed me and sat up bringing its feet up. The tourists finished taking their pictures. I then told it to 'hop it' and off it went. I was as surprised as the tourists were at its response to my commands and tone of voice.

I have even befriended swans; for years two beautiful swans had lived peacefully on the River Colne that passes through

Junia greeting Swanee

the park at Watford. They reared a family each year nesting amongst the reeds by the watercress beds, but suddenly tragedy struck; hooligans murdered the female whilst she was sitting on her nest and broke all her eggs. The cob was heart-broken; he would rush for shelter into the reeds if humans approached, and only in the early mornings and evenings did he gain enough confidence to come out into the middle of the river.

Those were the days when I always walked my Great Dane Junia in the park. Everyday I took bread for 'Swanee' as I named him and called him to me in my 'little voice' which birds and animals interpret as one of deep understanding. He came to me hissing rather rudely at Junia, so at first I made her lie down a short distance from the bank. Daily he grew tamer and tamer and his fear of Junia went; he would now take bread from my fingers, and learned not to snatch it, for swans have sort of teeth on their beaks which can really hurt if they grip one's fingers.

A few weeks later he knew me so well that, on my call, he would take to his wings if he was at any distance and land like a seaplane at my feet sending up a spray of water as he stopped right near the bank. Junia and he now greeted each other with a friendly sniff and much tail-wagging.

It was not long after we had become real friends that a female swan suddenly appeared on the canal which runs parallel with the river, about seventy-five yards away. She also looked lonely and frightened, and I decided these two must at all costs be brought together. Why they couldn't meet naturally with so little distance separating them I never quite understood, but they certainly did not meet that way.

Every day I brought two lots of bread one for Swanee and the other for the lone swan. She was very shy and hated dogs, who knows, perhaps a dog had at some time attacked her. I had to throw the crusts quite a distance into the canal before she would pick them up, dowse them in water and eat them. One needs enormous patience, a soothing tone of voice and a deep love for all creatures to be able to make friends with swans. After a few weeks I had both swans completely tame with me and Junia; they would I think have followed me on my walk if I had coaxed them to and this is what I set out to do. I got Swanee as he was the most biddable of the two to follow me right out of his river and over to the canal, and then gave him a shove. Before he knew what was happening he was swimming in it. The female was not in the least bit interested and moved off haughtily, but the temptation of their morning and evening tit-bits was too much even for her, and twice a day they both fed out of my hand.

One day the female wasn't there and I was heartbroken, had she decided to go back to where she had come from or had some

OVERLEAF *Introducing myself to a strange heifer*

tragedy befallen her? Swanee fed as usual, but he was not as happy on the canal as he had been on the river, so once again I tempted him back to his river, where by now although he no longer feared passers-by, he always kept his distance from them. I had never seen him go to anyone else for food.

I was feeding him one morning and called in vain for the other one, when suddenly there was a rush of wings and the lovely humming noise swans make when flying, and there was the missing female heading downwards straight for us. She came right up, took her bread and allowed me to stroke her head and Junia to sniff her in the accustomed friendly fashion. The swans stayed together all that year and in the late spring the pen was missing but Swanee had a proud confident look and often disappeared himself, only appearing out of the mass of reeds to take the bread I offered him. Then it happened – one morning I saw five beautiful baby cygnets swimming in formation behind Swanee and his pen. I called the swans to me for their food but it was the cygnets who reached me first, as if their parents had already told them I was their friend. I know this is nonsense, but I turned to a completely strange man who was passing me in the park and told him this was one of the happiest days of my life, and I felt as proud of those babies as if they had been my own. I am sure he thought me quite mad!

OPPOSITE ABOVE *Juno greeting a calf on holiday in Guernsey*
BELOW *Exchanging greetings with a tapir for 'Barbara Woodhouse's World of Animals'*

Mixed blessings

What an extraordinary thing a telephone is. I would say it was the biggest curse, and the biggest blessing of our lives. More amusing, annoying, devastating pleasureable and hateful things have happened to me with the use of the telephone than I think with any other inanimate object. The first time I ever used the telephone was when I was about five. I remember it had just been installed and I had to stand on a chair to reach the instrument. The excitement of turning the handle to call the operator (do not forget this was in 1915), and the tongue-tied way I gave the number of the little girl I wished to speak to was quite an adventure. When she answered, I could not think of anything to say, which is very far removed from what I have to say to many people on the phone today. It is an intrusion into privacy, as people can call one's house at any time of the day and night and they have got you at their mercy whether it be of importance or not. The telephone can be an absolute nuisance with, at present, children ringing, shouting 'walkies' and hanging up. I have tried having my telephone ex-directory but it puts off the people that I like talking to or who are in trouble and need my help, so I have gone back into the directory. I feel the cost of the telephone today is a great hardship to senior citizens whose only contact it is with many of their friends.

152

Hundreds of people a year ring me. I never mind giving advice but I seldom receive a grateful letter from any of the people I have helped on the phone. They usually start off by saying that they have borrowed my books from the library, from which the poor author gets no royalty at all, but I swallow my feelings about this and think of the poor dogs they are asking about, hoping I can be of use to make their lives happier. I know, however, that any advice I give on the phone will be pretty useless because many, very often, only want confirmation of their own ideas. Only by seeing me handle their dogs and seeing for themselves how dogs prefer firm but loving handling to weak and soft commands from their owners, will they learn how to get the best out of their dogs. My phone calls do not stop at requests for information about doggy subjects. A lady rang the other day to ask me if I knew of a flat where she and her daughter could live. A man rang and said he was a freelance photographer and could I tell him where he could find a stack of logs to photograph a model on. Why me? But the major number of phone calls are those I make, or do not make if the telephone is in its obstinate mood, which means I dial at least three times for every number I want, and the result is usually at least two blanks, one scream, one wrong number and an unobtainable, ending up with a call to the engineers who recognize my voice without my having to give them my phone number. This phone has been cursed. The number of times it has been re-wired and tended by the engineers is unrecorded, but it must make a world record. Once I dialled a London number and got Hamburg.

I always get on to other people's lines. I nearly always end up having to ask the operator to get me the number and put up with the annoyance of being asked if I dialled 01 in front. I think this is the arch insult of all when one has been striving for fifteen minutes to get through. I cannot think why my reasonably educated voice does not give the operator a clue that I would hardly omit to do this. Actually I know it is not the operator's fault, that it is something they have been told to ask, but how much better if they would assume you are not a congenital idiot and say 'You did, of course, dial 01'. It is a much more tactful way of approaching the subscriber. I think I must ask the telephone manager to do this. Talking about telephone conversations, one of the most amusing I have had was when my second baby was imminent. I got so bored waiting for her arrival that I decided to have a chat between pains with my sister which meant a long-distance call. The operator could not get a line easily and we started chatting. Before getting me the number, he asked if I could meet him the next day. I was most flattered but tactfully told him that it was not a very good moment to ask for the doubtful pleasure of my company. My husband who was in the room with me was most amused. I find that while waiting for calls, one can have quite amusing conversations with telephone operators. Years ago, when we lived at Stoke Mandeville, the local exchange was very much a personal village one and we got tremendously friendly with the lady who manned the switchboard. If we wanted to go to the cinema, she would take messages for me and knew all my business intimately. Unfortunately, all these little niceties of life have gone in the vast telephone system of today, and the fiend torments one with its inefficiency. I wonder how many telephones actually get thrown at the wall in a year? I have often felt like doing this. I must say telephone engineers must have undergone a period of politeness training before they take up their roles visiting people's homes. They always seem so tactful and soothing and leave with such smiles on their face as they announce the phone is now in order. Alas, the 'in order' sometimes only lasts until their van has disappeared down the road and one has to dash to the nearest phone box once again to call them back to give one a dialling tone, or disconnect one from some pair of interminable talkers to whom one's number has become hitched. We used to get all the railway station enquiries, because our number was near to that one. It kept me fit rushing to the phone from the garden, but it was infuriating for the caller and me. The telephone however is not, as far as I am concerned, the only piece of machinery that is cursed. I avoid wireless and television sets like the plague for directly I get too near them they refuse to work.

Ireland was my birthplace at a time when potatoes were still planted and harvested by hand, when fairies were still believed in, and when silver was put under the mattress in a thunderstorm in case it attracted lightning, and where, in my childhood days, the 'natives' did not believe in new-fangled ideas. All my life I have milked cows by hand, breathed up horses' noses to tame them, and have learned that it is the touch of my fingers and the tone of my voice that makes dogs behave, so perhaps it is of no wonder that I am cursed by machinery. I never come in contact if I can help it with motor mowers or they quietly pass out, and at first I thought that when the projector suddenly stopped at a showing of my films to an audience, it was just that the local shop had sent a dud one. I had to keep talking to the rather impatient audience instead of letting them see the films they had paid to see, so that the projectionist could go back to his shop and bring another projector. He arrived all puffed with the exertion of hurrying and set up the new projector. It absolutely refused to function and the audience left without having seen a foot of film.

My next experience was in hospital when I realized I had nearly been operated on when half conscious because the anaesthetist had been more overcome by the anaesthetic machine than me, due to some technical fault in the machine.

I ignored the trying time spent in a tunnel when the train I was travelling on suddenly drew to a halt and did not get going again for a very long time. I tried not to connect it with myself when the Bakerloo train refused to leave the station as soon as I had boarded it. But the great truth dawned on me that I had nurtured a curse on everything mechanical.

We bought a new fridge and set it up; it did not work. I had already told the salesman I thought the fridge might not work in my home and he laughed, thinking I was joking; only after his electricians had spent two hours trying to make the motor work did he begin to believe me. Four further models arrived at intervals and were taken back to the factory where they instantly worked on being plugged in. The fifth worked in my home as I went out the day it was to be installed.

Next we needed a new motor for the central heating. I warned the firm I had ordered one from that it might not work; the engineer who brought it to be installed thought I was mad. He pressed the switch to start it up and there was an ominous silence. Urgent phone calls were made to the chief engineer in London, the motor was taken to pieces and put together again but still showed no sign of working. A van fetched it back to the factory where it started up instantly. Three motors later and the last one worked – again I kept away.

Some years ago I wanted to make a short film on dog training. I warned the firm who were going to do the filming to check everything possible in their camera. The dogs behaved perfectly, even the owners seemed on their best behaviour, then after only about fifty feet of film had been shot the cameraman said apologetically that the camera had a fault. The sun was gradually going down over the horizon so filming became urgent. The dogs started going to sleep or fighting and the owners' gossip became ominously fretful. We filmed about one hundred feet then called it a day. Next morning the film laboratory phoned to say the film was a failure, some obscure fault in the camera had left ninety per cent of the film blank. Despondent but not yet feeling like giving up, I engaged another film company. The owners and dogs had to pretend they were quite new to the training and as the day ended and we sent the film to be processed, we all heaved sighs of relief. I could hardly believe my ears when the laboratories phoned to say almost the entire film was blank. I then looked at the third company's efforts after seeing the thumbs down sign as I entered the viewing theatre. At least, some of the material was usable. I decided to join together the usable parts from the three shootings and see if I could salvage anything that would make a short film. A sympathetic editor offered to lend me his cutting room and movieola so that I could view what remained from the three days' shooting. I warned him I thought I might render his movieola useless, but he just ignored me. It worked for about ten minutes and then slowly ground to a halt. He got it going again and we viewed a bit more film and then it gave up the ghost. I never completed the film – the money had run out.

Just recently, a magazine reporter asked to interview me with a photographer who was coming to take photos. The photographer took dozens of photographs – I warned him his camera would probably not work with me as his subject but he ignored my warning. When they packed up their things and left, I heaved a sigh of thanksgiving, thinking that perhaps my curse had vanished. Twenty minutes later a car drove in again and a downcast photographer admitted the camera had been faulty. I had to put on the fixed smile at the angles that the photographer wanted, and, at long last, he left again. To this day, I do not know whether the second batch of photographs were a success as I have never seen anything from the magazine even though I have a press cuttings agency. I fear the worst.

Two reporters came to interview me with tape recorders both of which refused to work and I got one well-known reporter, Ruth Wishart, to sign a statement to this effect so people know I am not inventing this.

Letter from Ruth Wishart

29.7.80.

This will certify that my tape recorder – with new batteries – came to a complete halt when placed near Mrs Woodhouse.

Ruth Wishart

OVERLEAF *Dodie, one of the stars of 'Training Dogs the Woodhouse Way'*

157

Apart from this curse on machines, we also share our house with a poltergeist. We built Campions on land that according to seventeenth-century deeds, had been granted common rights by the Lord of the Manor in 1675. The land was then known as Barnfields and given to a serf who could keep his cattle and sheep at nights on the land, and let them graze on the common at Croxley in the Manor of Croxley, and on common moor some two miles away. When I had a guernsey herd I grazed my cattle on the common, watching them from the vantage point of a stool with my typewriter on my knee, writing a book. According to the deeds I could have taken turf from the land, and it also entailed fishing rights in the river that runs through common moor. There were about twenty-five commoners in the early days, but bit by bit they have sold their houses and the commoners' rights have dwindled. It is only possible to have common rights upheld if you have what is termed 'couchant and levant' meaning that you have adequate pasturage for your animals which have to be kept on your own land at nights. They were usually stabled at nights in the olden days. The land must not in any way be fenced where there is common grazing. The freehold in our district was bought from Caius College, Cambridge, who were Lords of the Manor in the olden days, by the Rickmansworth Council, and whereas in the early fifties we commoners used to make hay of the common grass and flatten out the mole hills, the Council now, with our permission, cuts the grass with modern machinery, and in my opinion the lovely wild look, wild flowers and grasses of the common have been spoilt as a result. I did, however, get them to leave one area which is a mass of harebells in summer so at least we have memories of former beauty.

It was on half an acre of this ten-acre holding originally given to a serf by the Lord of the Manor, that we built our present house. Even in those olden days, the right to build one house and appurtenances was written into the deeds of the owners of the land. We feel this land in very ancient days must have been a burial place, for we have been left with a very

Our present home, Campions

annoying poltergeist who makes our lives a misery by taking away the things I want most at the very moment I need them. What is worse, it never brings them back if I look for them, which is very hard not to do when it is something important.

I remember putting a beautiful old parchment laying out all my common rights into a large envelope in the Westminster Bank. It was duly sealed and signed by the bank and me. When I went one day to get it out there was nothing in the envelope. The manager at the bank and I could hardly believe our eyes. It has never turned up. Luckily I have most of it in the main deeds. The poltergeist plays its tricks on anyone who lives here. My son thought I was going senile and grew quite annoyed when I complained the poltergeist had taken something. One day, however, he was the victim of its pranks. He received a cheque for two hundred and fifty pounds and put it down on his desk, as I do with my correspondence, and the 'ghost' as we term it, took it. We searched and searched but did not find it, so he had to have the cheque cancelled and another one sent to him. The thing faded from our minds until a year later, almost to the day, the cheque was returned by the ghost on his desk in exactly the same place as he had originally put it.

Everybody congratulates me on my prompt answering of all letters and dispatch of parcels. Little do they know I am spurred on by the 'ghost', for I have had letters taken from my hand when actually answering them and not brought back if I search too hard, but if I ignore the prank they will nine times out of ten be put back where I had them. My housekeeper did not believe in the ghost at first but now has to admit it exists. However, she is not a worrier like me, and the ghost brings her objects back quite quickly.

I went to stay with my sister in Derbyshire and, as bad luck would have it, my ghost decided a change of residence would be pleasant and followed me to her house. Some silver fish knives and forks were stored on the top shelf of the cupboard where I hung my clothes, and after I had left, my sister discovered they were missing. Hunt as she might there was no sign of them so I told her of my ghost and she gave up looking. Almost to the day, a year later, the fish knives and forks were back in their place on the shelf of the bedroom wardrobe where they had been when I used that room and had seen their case.

It is very wearing to live with a poltergeist such as we have, but in the end you just adapt your way of life to its antics. I know of no way of beating it at its own game.

Another mixed blessing that I find rather useful at times, is my gift for getting people to phone me by sending out a 'think'. I remember once I wished to speak to a man I had only seen about three times in my life. He was a courier for a travel agent, and I had only met him casually through his reading one of my books. I sent out a 'think' about ten o'clock one night, but got no response. I thought I must be slipping, but the following morning at eight thirty, the phone rang and this man said 'I only arrived in England late last night having been half round the world, but I had a feeling I had to ring you'. I told him I had been sending out a 'think' as I needed his advice and that is why he phoned me. He understood as he was a great animal lover and we all know animals communicate by telepathy. Another example of this was even more extraordinary. My son was looking for a job and had a lot of future interviews to attend. One day he went with some friends to watch the tennis at Wimbledon. At about two o'clock in the afternoon the phone rang and a lady from a big firm asked to speak to Patrick. She said someone had fallen out of an interview with their selection board that afternoon and, if Patrick could be in Victoria by four thirty, he could take the man's place. I said I would get in touch with him believing that if I rang Wimbledon, they would put a message out on the tannoy for me, but they refused. They said this facility was only used for life and death messages. I told them I thought an interview was life, but still they refused. How was I to get in touch with Patrick? If I drove over I would probably never find him as I did not know which court he was watching, so I sent out a desperate 'think'. Ten minutes later Patrick phoned me and got to the interview. This must be more than coincidence. Hundreds of people in my life have told me that they had their hands on the phone to call me as I called them – it cannot all be coincidence.

Nobody knows what a peculiar gift telepathy is. Sometimes it can be extremely advantageous, at other times it causes one to be excessively worried. One picks up thoughts of people and animals one knows to be miles away. One also seems gifted with a sort of second sight which I suppose is tied up with telepathy to a certain extent.

During the war, I knew exactly when my brother's face was slashed by a hawser on his Bren gun carrier. I remember now that I was in the middle of lunch when I suddenly said, 'Oh Bobby has been hit', the second it happened. I used to diagnose what was wrong with my husband's patients when he was a G.P. the moment I picked up the phone to answer their request for a visit from him. I was lecturing a club once and was explaining how I knew what was wrong with animals the moment I came in to contact with them without even examining them, when a lady asked me if it was the same with humans. I replied, yes, but to a lesser extent, so she asked me what was wrong with her husband and, without hesitation, I told her 'cancer of the jaw', which was right. I had just picked it up by telepathy from her. Yet I am certain if I was to be tested in this sort of thing, I would not be able to do it. I am inclined to interrupt people when they are talking to me, a very rude thing to do, but then you see I know exactly what they are going to say so it is a waste of time to let them say it all, but it is something I must stop doing. I know what animals are thinking and it has helped enormously with breaking in horses or training dogs, for one can anticipate and stop actions which might be harmful. I often ask people, 'Can you not see what your dog is going to do?' but they apparently cannot which always seems queer to me.

I have had some horrible experiences. I stopped my husband going on a train that was involved in a train disaster because I picked up that he would be in danger if he did. I also told my husband that if Patrick, my son, who had never rallied, went on a rally one Sunday, he would crash, 'Could I stop him going?' My husband said we must not stop Patrick doing what he wanted to do in spite of my second sight because he might feel I wanted him to consult me about everything he was going to do. At that time, he had had no plans to rally but someone dropped out at the last moment and Patrick took his place. During the rally he met another car head-on, in his Landrover, on a narrow bridge and Patrick went over the bridge and into the ditch. His Landrover was a complete write-off but he was only superficially hurt. Who was right? As it turned out we both were. I, in my second sight, my husband, in saying we must not stop him, because Patrick probably learned a lot about driving and he was not hurt, but I doubt if I would ever have forgiven myself for not using the gift I had been given if he had been seriously injured or killed, although I think I would have known the risk beforehand. That is why I say it is a devasting gift.

On the other hand, I have been able to help terribly unhappy people with it. I was at a wedding one day talking to a married couple. A few days later the wife (whom I had only met at the wedding) rang me up in floods of tears saying her husband had had a very bad stroke and the hospital did not think he would recover. I had told her at the wedding about my second sight and so she had rung me to see if I could be tuned in to her husband. I told her with the utmost confidence that the hospital was wrong and that her husband would get well. She rang me quite a number of times and when her husband came out of his coma, he rang me himself from his bedside phone to thank me for the help I had been to his wife in her worrying time. I do not know how I knew but I did. Not always is the outcome of things so happy. A lady doctor whose dog was a pupil of mine rang me up one night and we chatted. As I put the phone down I said to my husband, 'This is the last time I shall talk to her, she is going to die' – Forty-eight hours later she died. I told my husband Apollo 13 was faulty the day it set off and it proved to be. Just recently I travelled to Edinburgh on a Trident and, directly I got on the plane, I told Michael that I thought the plane was not right. She got off the ground very slowly and after we had been flying for about half an hour the pilot apologised for being a little late and said they had had trouble after take-off. How did I know?

Backache for beginners
and the funny side of the National Health

Thousands of people, nay millions of people today, are going around groaning, nagging, imploring, aching, cursing and resigning themselves to the fact that day and night they are caught up in wires and chains by a simple part of their anatomy, termed in the medical world as 'an intervertebral disc'. These small pads act as cushions between each vertebra, and can cause even heads of state to be at the mercy of all and sundry, for make no mistake, a displaced disc or even a replaced disc can give its owner such pain that all mental stability disappears while the pain rages and locks the human frame in positions that are neither elegant nor comfortable.

Pills by the ton are taken to alleviate the raging torrent of pain. Plaster jackets hold rigid the human frame that Nature meant to be supple and bending. Braces, potions, plasters, embrocations, epidurals, faith healers, chiropractors, osteopaths, doctors, surgeons, all strive to put back and keep in place these enemies of the human body, the displaced discs.

Crockery gets broken in the home by housewives and their husbands, who suddenly get locked with a jab of pain so severe that the hand fails to hold what it should have held on to. Spasm can make the bending sufferer only able to get upright again by the painstaking and devious method of climbing slowly with his hands up his own thighs until an

166

upright position has been attained. It has been known for people to be so caught in the throes of spasm that they are unable to rise. I was once caught under a cow I had been milking and there I had to stay until my husband came home to pull me out and up. The cow had cast withering looks at me trying to impress upon me that however long I stayed under her she would not be able to oblige me with more milk!

Discs are always a common ground for conversation amongst males and females alike. No one realizes how much these annoying discs can influence the world. A whole conference can be written off as hopeless purely and simply because one or more of its members cannot endure sitting any longer on a hard chair, with his mental states impaired by a neck disc that sends shooting pains through the head, or gives one a 'torticollis' or 'head on the side' fixation that is not only annoying to its owner but distracts the attention of all in contact with the sufferer from vital matters. The 'ughs' and 'ahs' that come without warning from victims interrupt the train of thoughts and conversations.

People are well aware that money can be made out of discs. Old soft beds have to be got rid of and new firm bases bought – a great advantage to the shopkeepers and manufacturers alike. An astute salesman will watch the posture of his approaching customer and cash in with sympathy and ready knowledge of the type of bed needed by the sufferer. The words, 'many sufferers with lumbago swear by this bed' are enough to get the 'discite' ready with his cheque book, for hope springs eternal, and although every specialist in the country may have told him to learn to live with his discs, deep down in his heart he cannot believe there is no cure.

Patience is one of the most amazing features of people with discs. They go home after a manipulation or heat treatment and are told to return in three weeks' time knowing the pain is very little better, yet they are still willing to wait that length of time for any improvement. It is a wise strategy of the medical world to let nature do its work for them, if it possibly can, and 'time, the great healer' is on their side.

Every sufferer believes his disc to be utterly different from anyone else's disc. Although he will try throwing himself over the arm of a sofa, if told to do so by a friend who was cured that way, he does not believe it will work a cure on him for his pain is unique, no one else could suffer so much and still live!

Discs do extraordinary things. A displaced disc in your lower back can not only cause pain at the seat of the trouble but a knee can become excruciatingly painful at the same time, and the question comes up as to whether you have a displaced cartilage or ostearthritis, when in reality it can merely be a referred pain from the site of the lumbar disc. Arms that ache at the elbow do not necessarily mean 'tennis elbow', they can be referred pain from a disc in the shoulder area. Hands that have 'pins and needles' at night are not necessarily a sign of 'creeping paralysis', they may merely be caused by a disc playing its pranks. To know your discs is half the battle won! In time, one becomes so familiar with them, that it is almost as much an art as playing the piano to get them in again and working.

For years I have earmarked certain pieces of furniture in my home as 'disc jockeys'. I jockey myself about on the arm of the big sitting-room chair, or lie crossways over my bed and let my arms and head fall over the side in an effort to extend the stiffening spine and thus leave room for the disc to go back in. I eye large, unruly dogs with envy for I know that a jerk on the lead in a forward direction is all one of my discs needs to get it back into place; the suddenness of the assault does the trick. If I went to a doctor to have a manipulation, I would naturally be tense awaiting the sudden push or pull I was to have, but a big dog's pull is unexpected and in goes the disc.

Discs are not always the result of gigantic efforts in the digging of the vegetable garden any more than they are the result of turning over in bed. That is what is so extraordinary about discs, you can go to bed fit as a fiddle and wake up a complete cripple. In fact, many disc owners feel that bed is the most dangerous place of all, for the stiffening process that goes on when one relaxes in bed is all set to cripple one. The blankets may be too heavy to allow free movement in turning over and the slight resistance they give is the perfect medium for putting a free and easy disc out. A dream may cause one to inadvertently jump in bed, then, with a clatter, the whole set of unbalanced discs fly out. The loud reports with which these can be replaced have to be heard to be believed, an experienced pratitioner can put them in like playing C scale on the piano.

How do discs start? Why is this malady so common these days, especially in women?

I expect discs were always common. I feel sure the jousting knights caught unawares by their opponents got off their horses with discs galore, but as interior sprung mattresses were not invented in those days the natural remedy of lying flat on a hard base probably cured the sufferer without further trouble.

Nowadays physical fitness is part of a school's curriculum. Gymnastic mistresses force unwilling backs to be bent double so that the owner can touch her toes. Discs love this and out they go. On complaining, the girl is told she must do more bending to get supple. In addition, a little hockey, netball or lacrosse with sudden turns are the perfect media for displacing discs. On leaving school and marrying, the home is complete with every form of disc displacer; carrying heavy buckets of coal, lifting the too heavy toddler, spring cleaning, or merely bending and stretching for beauty can all cause displaced discs.

Men, of course, get them by just being men and doing the chores they have to do: pushing the car that has conked out, digging the garden, doing a rugger tackle, laying a carpet, mending a fuse in a ridiculous cupboard under the stairs, clearing the blocked bathroom basin with the screw fixed behind the pedestal so that quite fantastic contortions are needed to reach it; as a result the water may begin to flow but the householder will never be the same again.

Discs cause mental troubles too. Forgetfulness is the most common. Housewives who buy things in shops and leave them behind are nine times out of ten disc sufferers. People who push nasty shopping baskets on wheels are amongst the ranks of displaced disc owners, for they imagine that by using these they will escape further injury. However, there is one delightful disc that relishes going out when you push things, and owners of such shopping baskets would be well advised to change around and pull them instead, if they own such a disc!

Injections, manipulations, operations, heat treatment, X-rays and so on are all lined up in the fight against discs, yet once a disc sufferer, always a disc sufferer. As the doctors so wisely tell us we have to learn to live with our discs. Avoid, where possible, the things that put your discs out, and believe me, that means practically everything that makes life interesting. The only way to do that would be to live on a desert island, and even then a coconut would probably fall on your head and give you a prolapsed disc!

I myself have had my whack of illness and displaced discs but have come through it all. I believe in mind over matter. In fact, it is funny that I should have ended up marrying a doctor, for most of my early experiences with the medical profession were not very complimentary to them, with the exception of a woman doctor who was quite wonderful. She understood that when a person has animals to look after, one cannot go to bed and stay there until the fever or whatever it is has gone.

Once, as a young girl, I slipped a disc playing hockey. I was duly sent into hospital for a manipulation by a very well known orthopaedic surgeon. Twice he manipulated me under an anaesthetic. The first time I came round he told me to get up and walk. I told him I could not, I thought my hip was dislocated; he did not believe me, but it was. The second effort went well and I was carted off to the ward to stay the night, but an hour later I discharged myself – my animals needed me.

Another time I saw a doctor after I had fallen rather badly off a horse and hurt my back. He examined me, causing me a lot of pain. I remarked to him, 'I think I am going to faint', as I would not have liked to do anything like that without warning him. He thought I was hysterical, slapped me hard, and I passed out and fell off the examination couch on to the floor. I had warned him! I always try to do things in an orderly manner. I remember once I got out of the car whilst on holiday in Guernsey to do some shopping and inadvertently shut my finger in the car door, it hurt terribly but I did not say anything – I had to do my shopping, so I went into the shop, bought what I wanted and returned to the car to take the dogs for a walk. I was just about to start the engine when I said to my husband, 'I don't think I can take the dogs for a walk,' and passed clean out with shock from the injury. I think this sort of behaviour again comes from my early upbringing when only 'cry babies' cried if they hurt themselves. Nanny always said I never cried however much I hurt myself as a tiny tot. I think it was to show my brothers I had 'guts', but this trait has led me into a lot of trouble, because nobody ever gives me any sympathy. When I am practically dying on my feet, friends have remarked, 'How well you look'. I once had terrible flu and could not go to bed because the cows had to be milked; the result was that I permanently lost my sense of taste and smell. Nobody sympathises, they do not realize how much I missed not being able to smell hay, the wet woods or other things that I love so much.

I well remember the cruelty handed out to me in the maternity home where I had my first baby. I told them that, owing to my disc injury, I could not lie flat and requested another pillow. A starched and soulless nurse remarked, 'Only one pillow allowed in this ward', so for twenty-four hours I had to keep my head on the back of the iron bedstead and put up with all that goes with having a first baby. Not only that, but there was a heatwave on and I asked for the curtains to be closed to keep out the sun – this was also refused. I was told that sun and fresh air are good for you.

Another time, also after an accident playing polo, I was taken to hospital and as 'casualty' was full, they put me on a stretcher minus most of my clothes, on the floor of the adjoining ladies cloakroom. I stayed there for three hours because I had been forgotten. It was not until one of the physiotherapists came to collect her coat that I was found and seen by the doctor. My trouble is I do not look miserable enough. I always pull people's legs if I can to speed the passing of time. Few people can take this and they certainly do not think you are ill or hurt if you can laugh.

The last and funniest experience I had was when I went into a local hospital for a minor operation. I arrived and was shown into a vast ward of women and told to undress and go and have a bath and then get into bed. I told the nurse I had had a bath just before I came and she said it did not matter I was to have another one, so rather than argue the point, I toddled off to the bathroom, ran some water and cleaned the bath, which in its dirty state, would have given me more germs than I had, had I got into it, and then with a lot of gurgling water running down the waste, I left the bathroom. Nobody questioned me. But when I drew down the sheets to get into bed, the sheets were also far from clean! I called the nurse, showed them to her and asked her to change them. I also asked if the window above me could be closed as it was winter and I was freezing. She refused, so I told her I would then get into bed in my woolly boots and fur coat to keep warm. She walked off and I did just that, the sheets were already filthy so I had nothing to lose. The Sister came and, horrified, she said, 'What would Matron say if she saw you,' I replied, 'Nothing compared to what I would say to Matron if she came along.' At that precise moment who should appear but Matron, 'Gracious,' she said, 'Mrs Woodhouse what are you doing in here?' I told her and she hustled me off to a private room with an electric blanket so that I could happily relinquish my fur coat and woolly boots. She had just discovered I was a doctor's wife and I was given VIP treatment. But the funny part was when I came out of the anaesthetic, I was alone in another room and there was a lot of banging going on. In a few minutes, a pickaxe came through the outer part of the wall, and I found myself staring up at the sky while an astonished workman peered at me. Apparently whoever had put me in that room had forgotten the hospital improvement scheme was in progress. I immediately donned my fur coat again and rang the bell. A nurse appeared carrying a kidney bowl with someone's false teeth in it. I had to assure her that I did not have such things and I asked her to go and phone my husband to take me away. I had almost had as much as I could take in one day!

I am nearly always in pain with my wretched back but you get used to it. I remember once an old groom telling me about polo ponies, 'Keep 'em on the move if they have anything wrong' – he was right and I think it is the same with human beings. Keep on the move, do not sit down – that is the secret. To this day, old countryfolk have cures that the modern medical or veterinary world do not know about. Once, when one of my ponies had bad diarrhoea, an old farmer told me to put the pony in a field with yarrow which cured it instantly. Perhaps the cravings that pregnant women have is something of the same sort. One hears of the most extraordinary cravings. I craved mint sauce when my second baby was on the way. I ate mint sauce with everything, maybe that is why I can be so vinegary at times!

I am a great believer in homeopathic medicine as I am allergic to practically everything. It is so often a question of mind over matter and, if things get really bad, the best remedy is sleep. I have the perfect control over this from long practice, but my doctor husband always marvels that instead of using sleeping pills, I just concentrate and, by sheer willpower, go to sleep!

I have found the medical profession generally quite unwilling to listen to new theories and ideas that might benefit ill people. Unless one is qualified, one is supposed to know nothing. Yet I, for years and years, have been working on the theory that nervous breakdowns in some cases, are caused purely and simply by lack of sugar to the brain. This can produce all the symptoms of hypomania and other allied mental illnesses. I thought of this when I suffered with diabetes in the Argentine and was one of the few people in the world to be cured by a native Indian with a concoction made of twigs from the Sarandi Blanco bush, which is not available for others yet as it has not been traced. I noticed then, that when sometimes I gave myself too much insulin in error, I felt quite unbalanced. I have got several people to try out my theory that glucose can cure many so-called nervous break-downs, and one day I hope I will be found to be right. This is effective particularly with young people, like students, who overwork and burn up all their available body glucose. I wish that more people would try taking two heaped teaspoonfuls of glucose three times a day in orange juice and tell me the result. It could turn out to be enormously profitable for sufferers and their families.

I think under the National Health Scheme, doctors are far too willing to dole out tablets and pills rather than give up the time to listen more to the troubles of their patients. I am sure a tremendous lot of bodily ills, aches and pains are caused by nervous stress rather than actual disease, and what terrifies me most is that a lot of the modern so-called tranquillizers can in fact, in those people sensitive to them, cause exactly the same symptoms as the illness they are supposed to be curing. I have got vast amounts of written data about drugs. I am dead against drugs of any sort, and in this family even though it is a doctor's household, you can hardly find an aspirin if you need one. The pendulum has swung too far now; what people need very often is comfort rather than drugs. I know antibiotics are wonderful and their use has revolutionized the treatment of ill health, but I also watch with anxiety, what dope is doing to people. Slimming pills, pep pills and tranquillizers, are taken by a lot of people who would be better off with long walks, a kind doctor to listen to their worries and healthier food. Television, I am sure, has done enormous harm with all its medical programmes. If you read a medical book you are sure you have got every disease that is listed and I am convinced the same is true of television. Besides that, it gives one the impression that doctors are superhuman so that people are disappointed if they are not immediately cured. Doctors can only do their best. A lot of people now think that they should go and see a special-ist as soon as they have anything wrong with them. G.P.s do not inspire the same confidence as they used to when my husband was one. It is obvious that a kind nature is what people most want in their G.P. not a walking prescription book. I am glad my husband became a consultant. He had time to help people by listening to their worries and I am sure, judging by the vast amount of Christmas presents, big and small he received, that this side of his character was appreciated. I once worked in a hospital and was horrified at the disinterest shown to some of the old patients who were kept waiting for hours to see a doctor. I am sure things have improved a lot since those days, but I have still seen things that make my blood boil. I am well able to fend for and protect myself but what happens to those timid ones less able to do so?

News and views

How do I view the future at over seventy-one years of age? Lots of people ask me what I am going to do now. Well, I am not going to change. I am going to do everything that is offered to me, and that I wish and can physically do. I am going to take an enormous interest in what goes on in the world. I think if I had not taken up dog training and animal work I would have liked to have been a barrister. My mother always said that I should have been a lawyer, because if there is one thing I enjoy doing, it is having a really good argument. That is why I like chat shows on the radio, if I am given a bit of a challenge. I have always been able to respond with quick repartee and I hope that as long as my brain lasts and I do not get too senile, I can continue in this way. I go on *Any Questions* sessions at the local community centre to keep my mind fresh and I have done two *Any Questions* programmes on radio.

I certainly do not feel old at seventy-one nor does my husband. Life begins at seventy, I say! It certainly has for me. One question that is put to me many times a day is 'What is it like to find yourself internationally famous at your age?' Well, I do not consider myself famous. I think that I have become

OPPOSITE *Replying to some of my many letters*

well-known through my public appearances and numerous articles and talks, but I would not call any of that famous. I do not think that dog trainers are really in a category to become famous. The famous people are those like Napoleon who have really done something worthwhile in this world. I may have helped over seventeen thousand people to train their dogs and lead happier lives, but none of that constitutes fame.

It is, however, good fun to be well-known. Wherever I go now I am recognized. I was in a butcher's shop recently when a little girl, not more than two years old, saw me through the window and called out, 'Look Mummy, TV!' I was going down the escalator at Baker Street the other day and as a woman passed me going in the other direction she laughed and called out 'walkies'. When I got out at the station another voice called 'sit' and when I gave my ticket up, the collector leaned across to his colleague and said, 'She's on TV'. I was flying off somewhere not long ago when the pilot of the plane came up to ask for my autograph and said as he left me 'walkies'. I said 'I hope not' and we both laughed. On the plane the stewardess wanted my autograph. It occurred to me then how few people will confess to wanting an autograph for themselves. It is always for a friend or a sister or a young person. When I was mixing in the studios with people like Clark Gable, Gracie Fields, Alec Guinness, Peter Finch and many more as a dog film star's trainer, I collected two volumes of autographs for my daughter who was recovering from a serious illness. We look through these books sometimes and it helps to bring back some very happy and interesting memories.

One advantage is that I do get a certain amount of perks from being well-known. I went into a shop the other day and bought a dress. I handed my bank card to the assistant as you have to do these days and she gave it back to me exclaiming, 'Oh no, I don't want that. You are famous'. I hope my credit will always be as good as that. Whatever I do now, I find everyone is much more helpful. I wanted to talk to a features editor on a major paper the other day, and asked the secretary to put me through. I heard her say, 'Please sir, Barbara

At a signing session

Woodhouse – "Walkies" – is on the telephone'. The fame that I have been favoured with will not alter our lives at all. I am unlikely even to get an extra holiday as my work has increased so much, with letters and telephone calls as well as my publishing business which I run entirely on my own with my husband's help. I could not get away without being inundated with work on my return. I have no secretary and have little time to myself. I cannot understand why people strive and strive to have a lot of money. Money over a certain amount brings little pleasure. If one has the basic things in life with a little to spare for your near friends and family, that is fine. Personally, I have no wish to get myself a lot of extra things. I do not buy many clothes. As I have said, I do not go often to a hairdresser and can do most things myself, so what good would a lot of money be to me? I would rather have less work.

Juno helping to look after the twins

When we moved to our former big Campions we had to work very hard to get enough money to keep it up and to buy new land. It was the dogs who paid to have the cowsheds built to my specifications with their film and television fees, but we pinched and scraped in those days to keep the place going and educate our three children properly. Things were a little easier when I began to earn more and Michael too, of course, became a consultant not just a G.P. We had no financial backing. That is why it was so risky when I made films. Often they cost little more than two hundred and fifty pounds but it was almost more than we could afford.

Even if we had a lot of money today, we would not know what to do with it. Anyway there is no fun in earning a lot these days as the income tax is so high and you are not allowed to give it to your children. At one time we could have given the surplus of the amount we earned to our children, but with Capital Transfer Tax you are only allowed to give them about

£3,000 a year so what good is earning? Much better to have a bit of peace.

Ingenuity has always enabled me to make money easily with new schemes, though not all of them work of course. Many years ago I had the good idea of making washable coloured nylon dog leads and collars, long before anyone else had thought of it. With the help of a very old business friend of mine, I had the nylon specially dyed for me in Manchester. My German maid made five hundred leads and collars a day on our old Singer sewing machine. My husband used to stamp out the holes in the collars with a special eyelet machine and I used to wrap them in pairs and sizes and dispatch them all over the country. Then a firm cottoned on to the idea and as I could not get a patent, I was out. Now every show dog today wears one of these collars and leads, and I can do nothing about it. Another idea I hoped would make money was to write phrase books in foreign languages that gave all the household phrases instead of the ones usually listed. I sent my idea to several publishers who all turned it down so I decided to publish them myself. All went well except for the problem of the cover. The board cover I was recommended faded almost instantly and I had to pay the extra cost of getting dust covers made. Later we used laminated covers, but they were not so much in use then. I sold 35,000 copies.

As I have already said several times in this story of my life, I am old-fashioned. I think the code by which one's parents brings one up stays with one for the rest of one's life. Those that deliberately defy that code, are not the happiest of people. My mother spent endless hours teaching us things, which when we were young seemed tedious, but we always paid attention, and now in later life, I wish some of the youngsters today would be taught the same things. Here are just a few of the lessons we learned. Never to overstay our welcome when we were invited out, for example, never stay longer than six o'clock when invited out to tea and any hint, however slight, by a hostess, should be taken. I always remember a funny incident that reminds me of this. My husband and I were stationed in Melksham during the war, and, doing our bit, we organized a party for the lads from the anti-aircraft gun in a nearby field. They came to supper one night and stayed and stayed, long past our normal bedtime. My sister, Hazel, was visiting us and when all normal hints that the party was over were ignored, Hazel said in a loud tone of voice, 'Well, thank you very much, Barbara, for a lovely party, I must be going', a cockney voice suddenly piped up, 'But you said you were staying the night'. This completely defeated us and it was two o'clock in the morning before we got rid of our last guest. Had they had a little training when children as to how not to overstay their welcome, we would all have enjoyed our entertaining more.

Three other things which we were taught and which I still think vital, were always to thank for a present by return, never be late for an appointment and always answer letters by return. Nowadays no one answers letters for weeks, nearly everyone is late for appointments and some of the youngsters do not ever bother to thank you for a present. If a 'thank you' letter arrives six weeks after the gift has been received, the giver, if it is me, feels aggrieved. I, in my busy life, have bothered to remember that gift, and given time to buy it and send it, surely the recipient can take the trouble to give up five minutes to say thank you. I always say, just a postcard of acknowledgement is all I want. Being late for an appointment is a crime in my opinion. How can one plan a day's work if those you are supposed to meet are late. I feel so bad tempered if anyone keeps me waiting that I do not want to see them. I remember the editor of a magazine once made an appointment to see me and he arrived one-and-a-half hours late. I was so angry that, in spite of the fact that I needed the publicity, I told him I could not see him and that he must make another appointment and keep it. I thought I would never see him again, but I did, and after that he was always punctual. Nowadays it is positively non-U to be punctual, and people seem very surprised if one is. I remember telling a psychiatrist in conversation one day that my children always phoned me if they were going to be a few minutes later than they had said. He looked at me as if to say I should be ready to enter a mental home at any minute, and asked, 'You do not mean the whole family is punctual, do you?' and when I said 'yes', I could see he thought me a future case for his notebook! I feel it is dishonest to be late, you are stealing someone's time, it does not matter whether it is your firm's time or just a private person's time. To many people, time is still money, yet those who offend would probably never think of stealing goods or money.

One other thing I shall always remember Mother telling us, was to look someone straight in the face when speaking to them, 'The eyes are the mirror of one's soul' and if one has nothing to hide, then let people look into that mirror. In later years I have found this extremely useful when I trained dogs. Few dogs will attack you if you look them straight in the face. All dogs sense your love for them if you are looking at them with love, and most dogs sense that they have done wrong when you look at them with disgust. The expression in the eyes is the greatest help in animal training or making friends with animals, and I think it is the same with human beings. Eyes, I have often noticed, change colour when people are ill. The eyes of physically and mentally exhausted people go pale in colour and this happens with dogs too. A dog that is going to bite you shows the intention by its eyes changing colour. Few people notice this, but in my life I have had to, or I would have got bitten more times than I would have liked.

Lastly, Mother always told us to say sorry if we were in the wrong, and this is the thing I find hardest to do. To admit one is wrong is a personal loss of face, and I fear in my life I have often wriggled out of things when I have been in the wrong. The Irish call it 'the gift of the gab', and I reckon that having been born in that Emerald Isle, the little people at my christening gave me 'the gift of the gab'. I have used it to tick people off until they have been insulted at every word, then I have twisted it round so that if they are on the telephone, they ask if they can come and see me, and if they do, we have become the best of friends. I have a sneaking feeling that some people

Sit! Stay!

A kiss from my pupil

enjoy a good ranting and raving, and like you for it, but my fault is that I seldom take back what I have said. It is a trait that I should try and conquer, but it is so easily got away with by the gift of the gab, that I regret to say, even at my age, I still am often in the wrong without admitting it.

One of the things in modern days that I simply hate is bad language on the television and vulgar sex. I am sure if a play or talk was funny you would not need filth to make people laugh. Vulgarity in any form coarsens one. The old plays and films were good and funny and had nothing obscene. I now find myself listening to television plays in my drawing-room where words I did not even know the meaning of until I was middle-aged, are used. I feel that this country is going – not to the dogs for dogs are too nice – but possibly to some other more unpleasant animal such as snakes. We should pull our socks up before we sink too low. We do not have respect for ourselves. As my mother used to say in the old days: 'If you use filthy language, it is not the person you are directing your talk to who gets hurt, it is you, and your soul that is forever damaged.' If you want to keep a happy fresh memory of your days, then it is vital to avoid using this filthy language that is being bandied about in our country – especially on television.

You must be courageous and rely on yourself. On the whole people are good. If they would give of themselves, of their work, of their best, I feel perfectly certain that this would be a happier world. Do not count on anyone else. I was persuaded once, when my writing and books began to be known, to get myself an agent. I did. He wrote to me to say that he was afraid there were no offers for my writings and that he could not do anything for me!

It is easy to overlook those who have had bad luck in their lives. I have always given special attention to handicapped people, helped them to train their dogs, as with the deaf, the armless and the blind.

Take a leaf out of their book. Never take 'no' for an answer. Do not let people depress and cheat you, and smile and laugh as much as you possibly can.

I never go to funerals. I do not believe in fretting for someone who has gone to a better life and I think it is also a waste to send flowers. I can remember all these thoughts when I was driving behind a motor hearse not long ago. After a little while I realized that instead of the usual solemn speed, this vehicle was going at one devil of a lick. We flashed past some police and a group of traffic wardens and I could not help thinking that had I not been mistaken as part of the mourning family, I should certainly have been brought in for speeding!

Another piece of advice is never go to sleep with something undone. If you have inspiration, you must use it at once or something will stop you doing so. Luckily, I write as quickly as I read, but whether other people can read my writing I do not know! As I write, there is a film and television project afoot which will use ponies. I so want to do it as I am always associated with dogs whereas I have spent thirty years with horses, having in my girlhood broken in hundreds of horses in the Argentine, run a riding school, bought and sold horses and owned ponies. I told the publishers that I would only write the *Barbara Woodhouse Book of Dogs* if I could also write the *Barbara Woodhouse Book of Ponies*. As it turned out the dog book sold only a small amount and the pony book sold 80,000 copies!

What worries me most in business today is that some people seem not to care about breaking their word. If I say I will do something or give a price for anything, I stick to it and would rather lose on the deal than go back on my word; but dozens of times in my life I have been let down flagrantly and I still will not learn. I get little sympathy for my mistakes in trusting people: 'Oh, that's business, dear' is all I am told. Why should business be built very often, as far as I can gather, on deceit and lies?

Yet I have met a few absolutely wonderful people in the film business, one in particular, a quite small film distributor who for seventeen years made money for me and got every possible release for films I made on sixteen millimetres and had blown up to thirty-five millimetres for the cinema. When I met Eric

Romer, known in the film world as Sax as he ran Saxon Films, he told me, 'I will do my damnedest to get your films released because I like your enterprise'. I have to take fifty per cent of the earnings because I have to work very hard for what I get. If you can find someone else to get the films a showing at a lesser percentage, I do not mind in the least.' It was worth every penny he took, not only because of the business he got for my films, but because he is without a doubt, one of the nicest, kindest businessmen I have ever met. His advice was invaluable, his loyalty and sympathy to all my 'let downs' was perennial. Money cannot buy these qualities, they are inborn. I have never met anyone else in my whole life who gave me quite such a helping hand in show business so freely. It is a business where you come across hard-headed men whom you have to meet on equal terms. I loved making films but the fact that you are a small producer trying to get into a big man's world does not matter. Producers are not interested in giving a film a try-out to see what the public want, and in my opinion, today are stuffing filth down the audiences' throats *ad nauseam.* I am absolutely sure that audiences would love something clean and nice for a change. The wind of change from sex and murders is blowing, as my television dog training series and the *Sound Of Music*'s phenomenal success have shown.

There is still one thing I wish to achieve in my life, and that is to be able to slip immediately into conversation in as many languages as possible. My mother spoke six fluently, including Russian. I shall never achieve all this, but to me this is education, and until I can do something like this, I consider I am ill-educated, something I do not accept easily, otherwise I think I have completed everything I have wanted to do.

OVERLEAF *Greeting my friends*

ABOVE *A visitor welcomes me to a local fête which I opened*
LEFT *With friends*

OPPOSITE *A new pupil who, in his excitement, balances on only one leg*

Acknowledgments

The author and publishers are grateful to the following for permission to reproduce photographs on the pages indicated:

The BBC for the photographs of Barbara Woodhouse taken during the filming of her television series on pages 2 and 158; Barratts Photo Press for the photograph of Barbara Woodhouse with Patrick on page 130; Hugh Burke for the photograph of Barbara Woodhouse with Patrick, Judith, Chica and Juno on page 105; the *Daily Express* for the photograph of Barbara Woodhouse in her office on page 136; Eastern Counties Newspapers Ltd for the photograph of Barbara Woodhouse with Juno on page 96; David Hobbs for the photograph of Barbara Woodhouse with Bernie Winters on page 116; Home Counties Newspapers Ltd for the photographs of Campions and of Barbara Woodhouse opening a fête on pages 65 and 188; Pictorial Press Ltd for the photograph of Barbara Woodhouse with Juno on page 62; Picture Power for the photograph by Bill Zygmant of Barbara Woodhouse with a tapir on page 150; Arthur Steel for the photographs of Barbara Woodhouse with pupils on page 184, and of Barbara Woodhouse in her garden on page 177; the *Sun* for the photographs of Barbara and Michael Woodhouse on page 100 and of Barbara Woodhouse 'with friends' on pages 140 and 188; Syndication International for the photographs of Duke, the Dulux dog, on page 72 and of Barbara Woodhouse with a pupil on page 189; Mrs Joyce Whitehead for the photograph of Saku and Tai on page 120; Michael Woodhouse for the photographs taken in America on pages 74, 80, 81, 86, 87, 88.

If in any case the acknowledgment proves to be inadequate the publishers apologize. In no case is such inadequacy intentional, and if any owner of copyright who has remained untraced will communicate with the publishers, the required acknowledgment will be made in future editions of the book.

Index

Numbers in *italics* refer to illustrations.
(Barbara Woodhouse has not been
included in the index).